# CONVERSATIONS IN COLOR

# CONVERSATIONS IN COLOR

Exploring North American
Musical Theatre

## Sean Mayes

*methuen* | drama

LONDON • NEW YORK • OXFORD • NEW DELHI • SYDNEY

METHUEN DRAMA
Bloomsbury Publishing Plc
50 Bedford Square, London, WC1B 3DP, UK
1385 Broadway, New York, NY 10018, USA
29 Earlsfort Terrace, Dublin 2, Ireland

BLOOMSBURY, METHUEN DRAMA and the Methuen Drama logo are
trademarks of Bloomsbury Publishing Plc

First published in Great Britain 2024

Cover design: Rebecca Heselton
Signage © LiiLit/Shutterstock & revel.stockart/Getty Images

A catalogue record for this book is available from the British Library.

A catalog record for this book is available from the Library of Congress.

ISBN:  HB:     978-1-3502-4210-4
       PB:     978-1-3502-4209-8
       ePDF:   978-1-3502-4211-1
       eBook:  978-1-3502-4212-8

Typeset by RefineCatch Limited, Bungay, Suffolk
Printed and bound in Great Britain

To find out more about our authors and books visit www.bloomsbury.com
and sign up for our newsletters.

# CONTENTS

# FOREWORD FROM ANDRÉ De SHIELDS

Look up the word "conversation," and you will encounter monopoly definitions: "a verbal exchange, especially an informal one, shared among two or more people." But, if the word is researched, a shroud appears to retreat, revealing its etymology, the ancient meaning of the word… "conduct." Specifically, an individual's deportment when traveling among far-flung destinations, kin to pedestrian etiquette. As global distances continue to diminish owing to the invention of the wheel, more expedient means of transportation, the Industrial Revolution, and, most recently, Artificial Intelligence, "conversation" has evolved into nothing more than "talk." This insight is due, in large part, to my having tasted the walnut of cultural intuition you now are holding in your hands, *CONVERSATIONS IN COLOR.*

Full disclosure: I am an Artist/Activist, and it is the mission of the Artist/Activist to fill intimate spaces with enormous beauty. The intimate space we pursue is the soul of humanity, and the enormous beauty is the power of liberated knowledge. Of the one hundred fifty pages, containing myriad examples of right-before-your-eyes-revelations from eleven town criers, the experience of each conversation is enhanced by the reading of the preceding or succeeding essay. These are invitations to the seeking traveler to come in, sit down and listen to all the wonderful things we dream about that still are not, all the machinations and mendacity that accompany us on our journey. These conversations can be had only through surrendering to creator-endowed sensory indulgence, which possesses sufficient room for the eternal garden of diversity, equity, and the pursuit of happiness. Allow your humanity to absorb the feeling of strengthening, inspired by knowing, perhaps for the first time, that we all are creatures of life's challenges. Constant dynamic change is the flow of the universe, and the law of that flow is energy expressed in a cosmic explosion of color; colors that defy the supremacy of the seven primary hues to which our tired eyes have become accustomed and can barely differentiate.

These collected conversations are not devotionals; however, I invite you to read one and not be aware of an ever-so-slight adjustment to your default consciousness. And when that happens, your decorum is awakened—you are not what you do but who you are. *That* is conversation. Color is simply a filter, and the new paradigm awaiting us on the horizon needs us to know ourselves, then be ourselves and communicate with others who have made similar pilgrimages.

*CONVERSATIONS IN COLOR* declares that the whole world's a mirror, and—if when you peer into it—your imagination is ignited, then the whole world becomes a stage for each of us to investigate with decorum, guide with decorum, heal with decorum, negotiate with decorum, and embrace joy with decorum.

Dear One, if you are reading these words, take a moment and consider the four elements: air, water, fire, and earth. Now use a second moment to look up, beyond the blue of the Earth's atmosphere, beyond the heliosphere, beyond the Milky Way, yes, even beyond the fathomless depths of interstellar space. What do you imagine? Imagination is a tool of Destiny. Time is longer than anything. Live your life accordingly. Leave culture, conversation, and civilization intact.

Lastly, kudos to author/curator Sean Mayes, whose vigorously genteel probing resulted in a mother-lode of inspired thought for the reader to consume in easy-to-digest doses of data: from the overview perspective of Zhailon Levingston's rapturous transformation, when in Kindergarten he experienced a life-changing moment upon his first encounter with a computer; and Baayork Lee's Broadway debut at age five, just prior to her subsequent flowering as the keeper of the keys to the Michael Bennett legacy; or the Stage Management revolution fomented almost single-handedly by Beverly Jenkins to include not only skill and discipline, but also nurturing and spiritual sustenance; or the community building through music education that Linda Twine added to her toolbox as Broadway Music Director and Orchestrator; or Stafford Arima's work as a cleric for Canadian producer Garth Drabinski that provided him the foundation to create a career highlighted by his becoming the first Asian Canadian to direct a musical on Broadway (*Allegiance*, starring George Takei and Lea Salonga). No less exhilarating is Alex Lacamoire, whose career embraces playing keyboard-bass in his Junior High School band, to studying Jazz and classical music at Boston Conservatory's Berklee School of Music, moonlighting as an audition pianist, then winning 2008 (*In the Heights*) and 2017 (*Hamilton*) TONY Awards for Best

Orchestrations. Equally fascinating is Jason Webb's journey from Church to Theatre musician, underpinning his philosophy of service as healer and helper. Schele Williams shares an intriguing yet humbling experience of becoming a parent at age thirty-nine. One might say that motherhood left her breathless while teaching her that—an admirable career notwithstanding—she felt that she knew nothing. Now, according to venerable Socrates, discovering that you know nothing is the beginning of wisdom. So, good on you, Schele. Or, Kimberley Rampersad who in Grade 3 was cast as the eponymous heroine in *Goldilocks and the Three Bears,* and the indelible moment of feeling, "I am enough." You see, Kimberly had not been forced to wear a blonde wig. Rick Sordelet blesses the reader by bringing his First Nation reverence for life to his discipline as Director of Stage Combat, a set of rules encouraging honesty, integrity, and stamina while undergoing any task. And Interdisciplinary Performance Scholar Masi Asare, who declares her responsibility to be the best craftsperson she can be, to be always present and visible and to encourage the rising of women of color. May the Conversations in Color remain unbroken. UBUNTU!

ANDRÉ DE SHIELDS

# INTRODUCTION

For years now, I've had the longing to see a text in print that gives voice to some of the best musical theatre creative team members in our art and industry to share insight and thoughts of their journeys, their work, and their hopes for the future.

At the time of writing this introduction, the path in writing this text, producing its interviews, and arranging time with its interviewees has been a long one: approximately three years in length and, most presently, it has undergone the long journey through the Covid-19 shutdown. Isolation has helped provide lots of *time*—time for reflection and consideration. I am positive you will see how the insight these practitioners already have is magnified to extreme lengths by the time that they, and we, have all had with additional reflective time.

My original inspiration for this text was from a book I've had for ages on my bookshelf. I'm incredibly thankful to Lyn Cramer for creating her own book, *Creating Musical Theatre: Discussions with Directors and Choreographers*, which reflects a similar sentiment: a longing to get inside the brains of some of our foremost theatre makers. Where my longing was unsatisfied was in wanting to see this told from the perspective of *more* people who looked like me, or who might have shared similar experiences as me—complex, intersectional ones that are marked by their, and our, existences in the industry as people of Color.

This longing exploded with my own time in isolation—both in curiosity but also in availability of time to be able to make this happen. The Coronavirus shutdown also collided with our universal reckoning of acknowledging in real time the disparities that continue to permeate and affect our world, and the inequities that people of color face consistently. With this, our industry has started its own reckoning—at the time of writing this introduction, *far* from fully addressed or close to being over but, certainly, a veil pulled back that can no longer be drawn closed again.

This book has never *not* been relevant—it's important; it will continue to be relevant and important because of the people who speak in the pages to come. That is, indeed, the point of this book: while the experiences you will read will be so rich as a result of how unique every person in this book is, they—we—are ultimately purely dedicated, passionate, emotionally connected art and theatre makers. It is that essential truth which makes this book even more important to exist right now, and their stories and thoughts tenfold more captivating.

My methodology was to try and find an array of colleagues and friends who could speak openly about their thoughts and experiences. My attempt to create a healthy, broad, and encompassing selection of identity within this book is as imperfect as trying to quantify a spectrum of color—we exist in many forms and across a wide, beautiful scale of identity. However, again, the people who are within these following pages represent a beautiful selection of some of the best, diverse, talent and creative positions, not limited to directors, choreographers, music directors, orchestrators, stage managers, writers, librettists, artistic directors, fight directors, within the theatre industry. It is worth reading for that *alone*.

I hope you enjoy this text. I hope you can approach with an open mind and an understanding that this crosses cultural borders and, as a result, the way that identities in this book are discussed might resonate with the person speaking it more than it does with you. Some succinct examples include the difference between our Indigenous neighbors to the north in Canada, versus our Native inhabitants in the United States. Identity is multilayered and requires openness to be receptive to how people seek to describe themselves and to be identified. You'll find this descriptive fluidity of identity throughout the book in peoples' own voices.

I hope you enjoy reading it as much as doing these interviews has given me such satisfaction and assurance that our art can and *will* continue to be better.

Buckle in and enjoy!

# ZHAILON LEVINGSTON

 **Zhailon Levingston** is a Louisiana-raised director and storyteller specializing in the development of new plays and musicals. Credits include: *Neptune* at Dixon Place and the Brooklyn Museum, *The Years That Went Wrong* at The Lark and MCC, *The Exonerated* at Columbia Law School, *Chariot Part 2* at SoHo Rep for The Movement Theatre Company, and *Mother of Pearl* at LaGuardia Performing Arts Center. He is the co-director of *Reconstruction* with Tony Award winner Rachel Chavkin. Most recently, he directed *Chicken & Biscuits* at Queens Theatre. He is the Director of Industry Initiatives for the Broadway Advocacy Coalition and was the resident director at *Tina: The Tina Turner Musical* on Broadway.

**What was the journey like for you? Where did you start?**

I went to a performing arts elementary school called South Highlands Elementary Performing Arts Magnet in Shreveport, Louisiana. And I didn't go because my mom particularly saw an artist in me; it was because it was one of the few Magnet schools in the city, and it was the best school right in town.

I forget the exact statistic, but it's something like, if a kid isn't exposed to theatre by the time they're twelve or thirteen, it's hard to get them to be interested in it. So, I remember the fifth grade play when I was in Kindergarten. And that was the big deal at the school: you started doing plays in the second grade, but the fifth grade play was the big production. In my head, to me, it was as big as it could get. Obviously at that age, I didn't know what Broadway was. I had never been to a musical. I saw the fifth grade production of *The Jungle Book*, and it blew my mind that these huge fifth graders that I saw in the hallway all the time were being Baloo and Mowgli, and that I could simultaneously hold in my head that it's them. I didn't have words for it, other than just being thrilled by what was happening. And I remember there was an entrance. The two things that really electrified me, for some reason, was the idea that they could come from the audience and make some entrance where they walk through the aisle. I couldn't fathom that you could break the fourth wall that way. And, the kids playing both Baloo and Mowgli at this predominantly white school were both Black.

So, I think there was actually a sense of identification. At a super, super early age, seeing myself in that position was not an impossible feat whatsoever. Politically, I've always said more representation, more representation. But, in terms of the personal, I never felt like I couldn't see myself somewhere because I saw myself at such an early age. The second thing that blew my mind was just that the kid playing Mowgli actually had the diaper wrap, and was actually wearing nothing. And then you do the second grade play. And I had one line as the mouse, and then, in the third grade play, I had two lines as the bee. You know, every year it gets a little better. I was so happy to be there. Then, we would get introduced to these classic musicals in drama class every year. Whatever the fifth graders were doing, that was what we watched. So I saw *The Music Man* very early; I saw *The Sound of Music* very early. I saw *Annie*. All those classics I was exposed to very early before I knew what theatre was. And then, in fifth grade, we did a production of *Aladdin*. And I was cast as this kind of short, chubby Black Aladdin. It totally changed everything. That was the year I first randomly went to a computer to type in the words "broadway.com", not knowing it was actually a website. And then that really changed my life. From that point on, I was like, "oh, this is a thing that people get paid for. Great. Well, this is what I'm going to do."

**When you started off as a performer, did you always have ideas at every step of the game about the work and think that you might be a director one day?**

Yeah, I'd say I probably did for most of my acting time, but not knowing that that was the quality of a director. So it wasn't until college that I realized that not everybody does this, and it's maybe not even always helpful. [*Laughter.*] Then, if you're not careful, you try to manipulate other people on stage to get the performance that you know they are capable of. And, honestly, I think that's probably one of the main factors that takes someone from being an actor to a director: that awareness that you're directing people on stage. And that's not cool. I didn't get in trouble for anything; I was just aware that I was always trying to push people into certain directions. There would be some classmates who would get on stage and black out. Like, what did I just do? And sometimes maybe that would happen but, more often than not, I was always performing and always aware.

**When did you decide to go to New York?**

Almost immediately, because I associated Broadway with New York. At a very, very early age, in my teenage years, I took a trip to New York with my theatre group. And the moment I arrived, I was like, "I can breathe easier now." And I was a pretty afraid person. I mean, the things that I'm not afraid of, I'm really not afraid of. The things that I'm afraid of, I'm *really* afraid of. And I was able to, at a very early age, navigate the city. For some reason, my mom trusted me. I would say, "I'm gonna walk to this theatre and get tickets." She was like, "okay." That wouldn't have happened in any other state. There was something going on that both of us knew that this is where I was supposed to be. And so, yeah, New York. I always told myself that that's where you're supposed to go. When I graduated AMDA in LA, I said, I'm going to stay here long enough to get my Equity points, but as soon as I have Equity, I'm going to go to New York. And I assumed that it would take two years. And it took about three months!

After I did this show, *The Christians*, in LA, I got my card and then immediately moved to New York, with one Equity check left, in the middle of a blizzard, sleeping on a broken futon with some very dysfunctional people selling Broadway tickets on the street.

**That's a pretty solid moving to New York story! So you finished school, you're here in New York, and you're working selling tickets.**

And I'm auditioning. I'm working just enough to have time talk or money talk. Which is to say not working many hours. But what I felt very quickly, when I was getting all these auditions that were going to final callbacks, was that I did not have the stamina for the bullshit of being an actor. It had nothing to do with my belief in my talent, and all to do with my capacity for navigating it in the way that I would have to have navigated it. I wasn't going to grad school. I wasn't at a school where the industry was waiting on people to come out of that school like they're waiting for people to come out of Juilliard or Carnegie Mellon. Maybe now more so. But, back then, I knew that it was going to be all relationships, and just getting out there grinding, which is like a special skill of mine. Ironically, that skill is actually more conducive to directing. It's not that it's less bullshit in directing. It's just as much and sometimes more. My instrument is simply set up to deal with that in a greater way than it is to deal with what comes with being an actor. And so I used to tell myself, and have recently started to tell myself this again, that when I first moved to New York, that I was in the service of story under the direction of form. And that is what I told myself to allow myself to do whatever I want to do: just follow the story.

And in 2016, after the death of Philando Castile and Alton Sterling, I created this arts campaign called *Words on Light* where we would do guerrilla performance art all over the city, sometimes with theatre, sometimes in the park, sometimes at churches, sometimes with school groups, or organizations. We would use the performing arts and the visual arts as a way of bringing people into difficult conversations. And we would just show up. No one knew who we were. We would just show up so that people would know me as that guy who comes with the long twenty-foot canvas and does things. So, that was kind of my back way into the industry because, at the same time, a lot of people were asking themselves the same question. What do I do with this information? And what do I make? What do I organize? How do we move it forward? And though I was still really, really young, I became a person that people would come to, or wanted to be in certain rooms to talk about certain things. And then I could catalogue who those people were, what I could get from them, and the ways in which they could help me artistically as well. Because that's what I had to do. Although I was also in the community, the broader Black arts community in general, the way that commercially people started to hear about me was through this kind of advocacy work that I started to do. And then from there came a lot of new play development and things like that.

**Is there like a project that you say was a turning point in terms of becoming a director?**

I had probably started directing in general when I was in high school. I knew I had the eye for it. But I thought that you're supposed to act for a very long time and then someone tells you, "hey, now you get to [direct]." I thought it was some kind of progression. I think I always wanted to be a director. I wanted to be a choreographer, which I did a little bit of. I don't do it anymore, really. But I thought that that came with age. Once I had the moment I realized that it didn't, it was full speed ahead.

I had been doing it, and I remember in maybe 2017 or 2018, I was set to direct and choreograph two shows in Louisiana: *American Idiot* and *Joseph and the Amazing Technicolor Dreamcoat*. Ultimately, for logistical reasons I wasn't able to do *American Idiot*, but I had told myself that if I can do a show as big as *Joseph*, and with as many people that have to be on stage and direct and choreograph it, if I'm happy with it, that I will return to New York and not get a day job. Which is crazy to have said. It wasn't like I was coming from a job that was making a ton of money. I only had part-time jobs for the first two years I was there. And this is what I was saying I was never going to go back to. So I kind of put myself in a situation where I had no choice but to work. I had to have a very, very limited living standard. I lived in very tiny, small spaces and didn't buy new clothes for a long time. And I couldn't do a bunch of shit, but I was fine because I was working. But then of course, you get tired of getting emails that have words like "stipend" and "honorarium", and you have to take things to a new level.

**I think an awesome thing for our readers too, thinking about the sacrifice. We always talk about that and that the work that has to be put in and if it is something that truly fuels you.**

You don't feel it while you're in it but, in hindsight, you're like, whoa. Asking friends, can you Venmo me $10 so I can get on the train for the week? You know, I've been there for sure. For sure.

**You have a new piece that you're working on. Do you have a manifesto you live by or a creative process that you apply for yourself as a creative to get ready to do it and to actually execute it?**

Yes and no. Everything is different. I try to do things that scare me. And so even sometimes, when I'm just going in and doing a reading, I'll say, I don't remember how to do this. I think that there's a certain level of that that is actually helpful. My job actually is to be able to sit with that comfortably and create a space where people can sit with the feeling of, "I don't know what we're doing either." Oh, cool. We're gonna figure it out together. That's actually the job. Not to come in and know everything. So at this point, I've made peace with the fact that, a day before rehearsal, I'll feel like I don't know if I can do it. There'll be another part of my brain being like, okay, good, good. You're in charge, you're gonna be ready for this. I guess my main creed, and you probably heard me say this before, is *how* we make is just as important as *what* we make. I believe this politically, for obvious reasons, but also what's not talked about enough is the importance of that artistically. This is the way I work with designers. It's the way I work with actors. The way I work with anyone is the quicker I can get you to feel like the vision belongs to you, the quicker I can trust that everyday you're coming into work just to do your job. You're not waiting to see what I have to say. I'm here to create a space where everyone has their own individual artistic agenda that's under the umbrella of a very particular vision. And ultimately, what gets me to that specificity of work is the belief that if we focus on how we are in the room together as much as what we're making, then the audience will actually feel that. They will actually know that, subconsciously, instinctively—almost like a motif and a piece of music. That motif will come out over and over again, in moments where the actors really need each other. All the work that they've done to trust each other will be made manifest in the room, in the event. That is part of what's going to make the thing the event, is to feel like they are taking care of each other.

I noticed this with *MJ* when I watched it, which is part of why I love it. Anne Bogart said, and I tend to agree, that ultimately on a base level, for her, theatre is about "how are we getting along? How are the characters getting along with each other? How are the actors getting along with each other? But how are the actors getting along with the audience?" But also how the audience is getting along with each other. And theatre is this excuse to examine that.

Then, there are very practical things I do all the time. I always check in. We're always going to stand in a circle. I'm always going to ask how you feel in the day. I'm always going to throw in a prompt. For the most part, I'll always allow it to take whatever time it needs to take to get through things like that.

**I remember that coming in on (*The*) *Tina (Turner Musical)*. I love it because it resonates so deeply with how I like to approach my practice as well. It's the idea of, we all come to a space collectively, willingly. And if we can just take a couple of seconds to agree that any practice that helps us connect with each other, and ourselves, even if it's only for a few fleeting moments, can be the nourishment we need.**

It was really scary to bring that into the team and process. Because when I worked on *Tina*, that was the first time I was working on Broadway and part of working on Broadway is mainly just learning the culture of Broadway. The craft of it isn't much different than anything you're going to do on any stage, but you learn what the standard way of doing things is. I think the ultimate marker of an artist's success is their integrity, and I knew that I would feel out of my integrity, if I didn't do that. If I didn't ask if it was okay if we stood in a circle and checked in. Now it's something they respond very positively to when it happens. But I remember actually being terrified of bringing that into the space and thinking that I was going to be looked at like an alien.

**What was the process of moving to Broadway? Did it feel like a switch clicking in a different way?**

I was obsessed with Broadway for so long. I'm such a musical theatre nerd. And I think when you come from a place where you don't have as many resources around those things, that becomes the thing that propels you—just your pure obsession with the thing. And so, yeah, there's a ton of things I had to learn about working on a Broadway show. But none of it felt overwhelming, because it felt like, ah, finally. I can check this thing off that I've always wanted to do. It didn't mean I saw it as better than other work, because I didn't. But it was like, ah, this toolbox now gets to be full. I consider so much of my career as free grad school. The grad school of public. So it was like, oh, great. I get to learn all of these things. I need to learn if I'm going to continue wanting to be in this space. What was far newer for me was to be associated with early development: new plays, and new musicals, and how you take something from the page to the stage. Because I hadn't had that training at all. So all of that training was done publicly.

**Do you think that is going to be something that defines you as someone who does all the new stuff or does all the revivals?**

No. I feel I can't be defined by any kind of traditional theatrical boxes particularly because of the times we are living in. So I'm much more interested in how to continue to smash the notion of what can happen within those four walls. And the four walls themselves. I'm as interested in working with pop artists as I am with directing a musical on Broadway. I really want to direct the musical on Broadway. I also really want to fucking direct the Grammys! I also really want to make movies and film and television. I think that my journey is about developing Zhailon as a property that means storytelling. But I don't want that to be confined to between 42nd and 56th Street.

**How do you feel about being one of the youngest directors on Broadway, especially having that as an accolade that's been thrust upon you? Does that make you reflect upon anything?**

Initially, when you first bring it up in conversation, it's cool. But just cool. But the longer you talk about it, the more depressing it actually is. Because, statistically, the next youngest director on Broadway, other than the director of *Six*, who is essentially the same age, is not like a year or two ahead of me. We're talking about ten, fifteen years older than me. So that sucks. Especially when we're talking about Black directors, though. And I think me being the youngest Black director on Broadway says much more about Broadway than it does about me. But, you know, it's cool. I would be lying to say there wasn't a nerdy part of me that likes the fact of it. That there's a little arc that I made, but it's very hard to see the impact of it. Even now, I don't know what the impact of it is, or will be, or what it would mean. Ultimately, everything I do is for the person in Louisiana, Oklahoma, Texas, wherever, who I know is just spending their lives in front of YouTube trying to learn as much as they can because it seems so far away from them. And so if they are inspired by what I am doing, that means the most to me, but it doesn't really mean anything abstractly.

**Do you still feel an affinity or connection to Louisiana and down in the South?**

I think I'm inherently Southern. I think it just is what it is. And I think that finds its way in my work. I think it finds its way into my process because of the sense of community that I grew up around. But I think it also finds its way into the ways in which we kind of disrupt what we consider to be commercial theatre. I think it was Quiara Alegría Hudes who said that commercial theatre, theatre on Broadway, is predominantly straight, white, male, atheistic aesthetic. And obviously, I'm not straight, I'm not white. I am a male. But the other part that isn't addressed as much is that Black people in the space are going to disrupt this idea of the atheistic aesthetic. Which is, to me, a kind of centering of deconstructionist theatre, or a kind of essentialism when talking about things other than straight white men. It has to be essentialism because that's the only context that anybody has from those experiences. So I think that my Southerness brings in so many kinds of institutional practices that are indigenous to the south in ways that the theatre desperately needs.

**It's hard to believe, but we are, numerically, just short of two years away from George Floyd's murder and everything that happened in 2020. Where is your heart, mind, and brain at in terms of what we've done and where we got to go?**

Yeah, I think that I have no hope in the old model. Now, that does not mean there isn't a part of me, egoically, that would like parts of the old model to work. Because that's what we were promised. Is that it would work. And I just wanted to come and work. That's it. I didn't want my vocation to be about completely reimagining the entire machine. But, of course, that is within our tradition. And so, I have no hope in the old model, because I think the evidence is just overwhelming that it is in danger of extinction. But I don't think that means that the theatre has to be. And I don't even think that means it has to be extinct commercially. And I have tons of hope, in what I think is an inevitable shift to something more expansive, something more cutting edge, something more malleable and emergent. I think we all are on the vanguard of the folks who are helping to make that happen, even if you're just surviving every day. You're evidence of something about where it's all going. And what I know to be true is that, if you are an institution that is not going there, you will die. Not because you deserve it, not because you did something bad, but because literally we are evolving.

America was truly different after 9/11. Despite what you think about that event, America actually changed. And it took all that it took for Broadway to be confronted with itself. It's still being confronted. It has not changed yet. But, I think, almost an equally important stage in that change is to actually be confronted with yourself, be disrupted by your own patterns, and to learn from those consequences. I've told people that some shows, some theatres, some organizations, are not going to learn from these panels or workshops. Bodies are going to have to be endangered. Money is going to have to be lost for them to see it. For them to get it. And those are the places where the industry will never sprout back up again. And that's okay. Because it's sprouting back up—in other places as well. And so, we may have an industry where 42nd to 56th Street is not the commercial hub of theatre anymore, but it doesn't mean that commercial theatre will go away. And I think with this racial moment, and this world pandemic moment, people are wrong if they think that those are the things that are changing Broadway. What's changing Broadway is Broadway's ability to either adapt to these things or choose to not. That is actually where the change is happening. It's not that it took this to make it happen. It took that to reveal something about ourselves. Ultimately, it is us who have to make the choice.

**Do you think often about those coming up behind us?**

That's all I think about, honestly. I think about myself and I think about the people around me. But that's never going to give me the amount of self discipline that I need to keep going through how hard the times are right now. I think, if you're not thinking about someone who isn't here yet, I don't know what bigger thing there is to be thinking about that actually gets you through the days that are really, really tough sometimes. It's the hope that no one else will have to do it.

**Do you have any upcoming projects that are really rooting you in your love of musical theatre and some cool aspiration for where it's going?**

There's a few projects that I'm working on that do the thing that is the opposite of the kind of deconstructionist theatre that we're used to. Which is to actually deconstruct to a point where the show breaks open, and then to choose to keep moving forward. I think I'm interested in working on pieces that don't let the audience leave after understanding, but go from a place of unknowing to understanding to unknowing again, and reconstructing a kind of new way of being together. So, you know, there's projects that I'm working on with The TEAM and others. There's a musical I'm working on called *A Burning Church*, that doesn't just ask the question, what happens to these institutions when they fall, or what can make an institution fall, but rather, what happens to it after it falls? What's built in its place, or not built in its place? Which I think are the most vital questions that we can be asking as artists right now. We are living in an empire that is falling. And we will all have to figure out what to do with that.

**Is there anything else that you want to add that you feel like you haven't covered?**

I would just say, as a statement, I think it's really important that these voices are heard right now because I think what can so easily happen in our industry is that voices of color can be just used in a kind of encyclopedic way, but never be actually thought of as serious artists. I think that it takes us being able to talk to each other and promote each other's voices, the way we think and our techniques and what our thoughts are on our craft, for that to survive this time. Because, if not, we'll just be known as people who were there and not people who were actually contributing. It's like *Shuffle Along*. It being the split note in history as people who were there as opposed to people who actually changed the way everyone did everything afterwards. I appreciate the opportunity to talk past just what I think white people should do with themselves.

**Thanks so much, Zhailon.**

Yeah, thanks, Sean. This was awesome.

# BAAYORK LEE

**Baayork Lee** has performed in a dozen original Broadway shows. She created the role of Connie in *A Chorus Line* while continuing the legacy of Michael Bennett directing companies around the world, most recently Antonio Banderas' Company in Spain. She has directed *The King and I*, *South Pacific*, *Cinderella* (R&H), *Porgy and Bess*, *Carmen Jones*, *Jesus Christ Superstar*, *Barnum*, *Gypsy*, and others. She also directed the 2021 *Wicked in Concert* for PBS. Her choreography credits include: *Miss Saigon*, *Mack and Mabel*, and, for Arena Stage in Washington, DC, *Animal Crackers*, *South Pacific* (Helen Hayes Nomination in 2021), *Wicked in Concert* 2021 for PBS, *Coconuts*, and *Camelot*.

Lee founded National Asian Artists Project (NAAP) a 501(c)3 Nonprofit. Her vision includes educating, cultivating, and stimulating audiences and artists of Asian descent through the many outreach programs the company offers.

She has been the recipient of numerous awards for her work, including the Isabelle Stevenson Tony Award, Paul Robeson Award from Actors' Equity Association, the Asian Woman Warrior Award for Lifetime Achievement from Columbia College, Asian Pacific American Heritage Association Achievement In Arts Award, the Dynamic Achiever Award from OCA Westchester, Chen Dance Center Artist Award, Arena Stage American Artist Award, and Actors Fund for Outstanding Contribution to the World of Dance.

**Can you tell us about how your Broadway career began at such a young age?**

I've been blessed in my career. That's all I can say. Starting at five years old, my father had our Chinese restaurant in Chinatown. And the casting people [for *The King and* I] came down looking for kids, so we all went down, and I got the job as the original principal, Princess Ying Yawolak.

**Did you know at five that this was going to be it, Broadway was for you?**

No doubt about it. I saw the chandeliers, the red velvet seats, signing in . . . I loved it. I watched the dancers warm up with a ballet warm up. Yuriko [Kikuchi], who was one of the dancers, was my mentor. I mean, I just admired her and that's who I wanted to be, so I wanted to dance too. They told me that they were with the School of American Ballet, they came from the Jerome Robbins side.

When I was fired at eight years old because I outgrew my costume, I just knew that I had to study. I knew I wanted to come back. My mother listened to me! When I got let go it was at the same time as three other children, so Rodgers and Hammerstein asked the three of us what we wanted to do. And one wanted to be a pianist, one wanted acting class, and I wanted to dance. So they helped us a little bit, but Jerome Robbins also helped me get into the school. I was at the School of American Ballet for twelve years: I studied. And that's where Balanchine did his first *Nutcracker* that I was in. The next person that I just emulated was Maria Tallchief, who was Native American. I wanted to be a ballerina too!

In fact, even before I started with *The King and I*, my neighbor upstairs was a dancer with the Katherine Dunham group. And he said to my mother, we have a school and I teach there, why don't you bring your daughter there? So, at three years old, I was running around and listening to Katherine Dunham's drum at the Katherine Dunham School of Dance. At that time, Karel Shook was at the school teaching ballet. Shook was mentoring Arthur Mitchell [the Black ballet dancer]. It was funny, I was always getting into New York City Ballet at 8am, and Arthur was at the school as an adult. So my mother would give Arthur Mitchell a peanut butter jelly sandwich and, a dime. And he would take me to class.

**So were your family supportive in you pursuing a theatrical career?**

First of all, my father worked in a 24/7 restaurant. Everything was left to my mother, and I bullied her into what I wanted to do! My brothers torture me now saying, you know, "I couldn't go to a baseball game, I had to go get you from dancing school!"

**And how did you go from getting fired to your next show?**

Well, I got fired and I started getting technique in! And then I heard that Rogers and Hammerstein were doing *Flower Drum Song* and I went down, and Mr. Rogers remembered me, and said, "you want to do the show?" And so I got into my second Broadway show.

The day that I got *Flower Drum Song*, I was at the Seville Afford Studios. By then, Katherine Dunham had closed her school, and one of her lead dancers opened up her own school, and she became one of my mentors. So I went to the school after my audition, and Michael Bennett was there, and I said to him, "I'm gonna be doing my second Broadway show!" He said, "I haven't even done one. And she comes and tells me she's got two!"

I was Michael's first friend in New York. Years later, we found ourselves on Broadway doing *Here's Love*, as dancers for Michael Kidd. At that point Michael said, "I want to be a choreographer." And everybody said, "Oh, yes, yes, yes." Because at that time you had Michael Kidd, you have Bob Fosse, you have Peter Gennaro, all these, you know, older men in their forties. And Michael was only twenty. And he was saying he wants to be a Broadway choreographer.

At that time, you had to have a home, you had to have your team. Bob Fosse: he had his dancers; Jerome Robbins had his dancers, you know, everybody had their home. Michael Bennett said he wanted *me* to be a Michael Bennett dancer. And I thought, Wow, that's great. Because I had been hopping from Peter Gennaro to Michael Kidd, didn't have a home. When you had a home ... and you had a choreographer, you did everything: their television shows, their Broadway shows, their commercials—you did *everything*. So, for me to have to have somebody, was fantastic.

**The relationship with Michael Bennett is a big moment in your career and life . . .**

When we were doing *Promises, Promises*, I was singing and dancing and carrying on in the back. Michael came down and said our Dance Captain has gone off to do *Oh, Calcutta*, so you're going to be the dance captain. And I said, "Oh, I can't give your notes to Jerry Orbach!" I was a turkey lurkey girl! And he said that he would train me, and that was the beginning of my training ground for what I'm doing now. Michael was very specific, you know, he and Bob Avian [co-choreographer for *A Chorus Line*] really groomed me for what I'm doing. At the opening night of *A Chorus Line*, Michael gave me the baton and said, "You're going to go around the world, And, reproduce this." And I just went, "Oh, yeah, sure, sure, sure." Because I'm one of the authors, my life is in the show, I helped develop the show.

**Do you feel his legacy is still with you when you're working on the show?**

Yes, he's there, all the time. He's present at all my rehearsals and all of my auditions; he trained me how to audition. Because, *A Chorus Line* is very, very specific. Michael said, "When you audition, I want everybody to leave, whether they got the job or not, they must leave with something—with hope." And that is learning the combination so that, when they come back again, they know it, or the dialogue that we give them. I carry that with me, and also the process that he gave us in creating the show, which I reproduce. He's there with me all the time.

When Michael Bennett and Bob Avian passed me the baton, I promised the original company that we *all* collaborated on this project, and I would definitely talk about them and talk about their input. Forty-five years later, forty-six years later, it's still very, very fresh, very fresh in my mind. Because this is Michael Bennett's legacy and Bob Avian's legacy, and they left it for me to pass on. And so I trained assistants and associates to go on and do the show.

**How do you think about your own legacy when you're rehearsing?**

When you are in the whirlpool, there is no time to step out and look back. "Whatever this is, whatever you are, I'm doing it. I'm in the present." When I left *King and I*, Yul Brynner gave me a three-sided, three-headed white elephant, with two faces to the side and one to the front. And he said, "I gave you this because I never want you to look back." I was eight years old! He had no idea what career I would have. I go by that all the time. I don't look back. I've done fifty-something productions of *A Chorus Line*, I have no idea how many.

Don't give up on your dream. *Don't give up on your dream.* And you'll know when it's time to go and say bye! You got to give it that last try: don't go home yet. Don't get that ticket to go home yet. Let's just keep going to those auditions kids, keep at it!

**As artists of color, we sometimes have to imagine ourselves in the picture when we're not yet in it; we have to look at the picture and think, soon this will look more like me.**

You have to show up. You *have to show up*. And when they say no, you have to show up. And when they say no, you have to show up and maybe they say no. And then finally they say "oh my god, you've been here so many times. *Yes*."

**Come on in . . .**

. . . And you better be ready, when the door opens, and you can let your foot get in there. Because if you get in here, you better be good!

When *A Chorus Line* opened, my cousin said, "Be, you better be good, because all of Chinatown is depending on you!" So I knew very early on that my community was, if not depending on me, they were looking for me to make people more aware of them.

**Could you tell us more about your work forming the National Asian Artists Project?**

There was a point when I realized I haven't done any teaching for my own community. I was very lucky to be able to direct the *King and I* [in Atlanta] and the day after the show closed, I said, where are all these beautiful dancers and performers going?

Oh, they're waiting for the next *King and I*, or *Saigon*. And I decided to form the company. And that was the first thing I said, I want to do *Oklahoma* and *Carousel*. I was in Japan, and they're doing *Show Boat*, and *Les Mis*, and all of these things. And I said, "That's what I want to do here." So the National Asian Artists project is to bridge the East with the West.

And then I realized, you have to start educating them from the little ones. Yeah. I got the opportunity to go back to Chinatown where I was born and raised, and open an after school programme called Theatre Club at PS124. And we're there for ten years now, going on eleven years.

The most important thing is I opened up their minds, which is how I pitched the program. The students sing and dance, and they do monologues, so that when they get up in front of anybody at school, they can talk and they have more confidence. That's the most important thing. I don't want them to have to be in the theatre. They don't have to be performers.

**What advice would you have for those people who do want to be performers?**

Do your homework. Know who is in the room. What are you auditioning for? Study and continue. I know what I want to say. And I tell all of my casts this: We want to be artists. We don't want to be singers, dancers and actors. We want to be artists. And what does that mean? We go for perfection. And we continue to work on our craft. We are artists. That's what we achieve.

# BEVERLY JENKINS

**Beverly Jenkins**, recipient of the 2020 Tony Honors Award for Excellence in Theatre, has been a professional stage manager for over thirty years. She is currently the production stage manager for the revival of Bob Fosse's *DANCIN'*. A graduate of Howard University, Ms. Jenkins got her start on Broadway as the production assistant on *Five Guys Named Moe* and eventually became the assistant stage manager. She has since managed many Broadway shows; her credits include the revival of *The Piano Lesson* directed by Latanya Richardson Jackson, Tony Award-winning Best Musical *Hadestown*, *A Bronx Tale: The Musical*, *Fully Committed*, *Amazing Grace*, *Living On Love*, *Holler If Ya Hear Me*, *Machinal*, *Godspell*, *Bengal Tiger at the Baghdad Zoo*, *In the Heights*, *Shrek: The Musical*, *Avenue Q*, *Aida*, *Sweet Charity*, *Oklahoma!*, *The Lion King*, *Bring in 'da Noise/Bring in 'da Funk*, *and Miss Saigon*, along with numerous other productions. She has worked with Roundabout Theatre Company on *Bad Jews* and *If There Is I Haven't Found It Yet*, and at Paper Mill Playhouse for the regional run of *A Bronx Tale*. During her career in theatre management, Ms. Jenkins has been Production Supervisor for *Summer: The Donna Summer Musical* and *A Bronx Tale*, Company Manager at The Negro Ensemble Company, and Executive Assistant at Frank Silvera Writers' Workshop. When she served as Producer for the AUDELCO Awards, she had the pleasure of working closely with the organization's founder, Vivian E. Robinson. She toured Europe with Jubilation! Dance Company and has managed numerous special events and benefits. Beverly has served as Executive Director of the Black Rock Coalition and has taught at several universities including NYU Tisch School of the Arts and Shenandoah Conservatory at Shenandoah University. Ms. Jenkins is on the board of trustees of Broadway Cares/Equity Fights AIDS and Beyond the Stage Door. She is co-founder of Broadway & Beyond: Access for Stage Managers of Color. Most importantly, Ms. Jenkins is a wife, mom, daughter, sister, and friend.

**What about our current situation makes this book relevant?**

People of color are so in vogue that during the off time, or The Middle Ages as I like to call it [the COVID pandemic] Lisa Dawn Cave, myself, and Jimmie Lee Smith started an organization called Broadway & Beyond: Access for Stage Managers of Color.

**I remember coming across the idea because I was looking for somebody for a recent project!**

Absolutely. We started this organization because there were a lot of organizations forming in the aftermath of George Floyd, Breonna Taylor, and Ahmaud Arbery. And it was like, yeah, we're done with this.

**Yeah.**

It was a response to all the promises that non-Black people were making, saying, "We see you." Don't see me! Do some shit. Stop seeing me. I know you see me, and you keep going. So no, don't see me. Do. And so, in our business of theatre, there were a lot of organizations popping up that were about training people. However, there was a whole group of people who were being missed. And those are people who were already trained who just can't get hired because people who do the hiring don't know them. A few of us somehow slipped through and we were able to make careers out of it. Lifelong careers. For me, it's now thirty years doing this and I'm very grateful for every second. And so, we thought, how can we make this better? Well, someone else can train them. But there are people out there who are working who just don't know who to contact. And we believe that there are people out there who would love to hire, but just don't know where to find folks.

**I couldn't believe it myself. When I went to find a stage manager, I couldn't believe how few stage managers of color in this city that I knew of.**

When we had rehearsal, Jewelle Blackman [original Fate from, *Hadestown*] got my emails, and then she walked in and I'm like, "Hi, I'm Beverly I'm your stage manager." She was almost floored! She said, "Oh my God, she's Black." Because she had never worked with one before. She was like, "Especially the PSM? No, never." And I'm like, "Yeah."

**You know, you're the mom of the company.**

I am the mom. Absolutely.

We feel the difference here at *Hadestown*. Because there's a certain nurturing and understanding that you bring to the job that is a part of who you are as a person of color, because of what we have to do to make it through this world. Which makes you a different kind of leader. Have you consciously seen, felt, heard that to be true?

I know my brownness got me in the first door. Period.

**Interesting. What was that first door?**

My first door was *Five Guys Named Moe*. And it wasn't a secret. They were looking for Black stage managers. You had a Black director, you had a Black choreographer, you're looking for Black people. They actually put it out there.

**Who were some of your mentors?**

When I first started, the PSM was someone who I consider to be my PSM mother. She is a white woman, but she really nurtured me in my early years on Broadway. Marybeth Abel, who is currently over on *Wicked*, was the PSM. The first was Gwen Gilliam, who is the Queen, and the second was also the swing and dance captain in the show because you could do both back in the day. And his name is Roumel Reaux. And I was the PA. Solo PA. But I was also old for PA-ing. I was twenty-eight, almost twenty-nine years old. I was no baby. I had been travelling in dance companies and I had another life in the music business, but I booked that job. And I was like, this is fantastic. You know, I got in and I sucked up as much as I can and I learned and I learned and from there, not even two years later, they called. The same office called me and asked me to go over to speak to the stage management team at *Miss Saigon*. And I got hired as a short term. They had to fill in for someone who was going away for a few months, and that person never returned and I got the job. So I ended up there for a while, and then it just kept moving from there.

**What kept you in the door?**

My qualifications. If you can't do the job, especially if you're brown, then that gives people an excuse to say "we tried." With Broadway & Beyond, we really try to tell people you're not going to find a PSM for every Broadway show on Broadway because you haven't nurtured any in the last forty to fifty years. So, the few that you have nurtured, we're working.

Now, it's time for you to take somebody, hire someone to be the PA, hire someone to be the second, and let them get that experience. And then, ten years from now, come talk to me. You're going to have a nice group of qualified working brown, Black, Latinx, Asian people. Whatever you need, we're going to be there. We have similar conversations with MUSE [Musicians United for Social Equity]. The biggest thing is that people are just in such disbelief but, internally, we recognize there's only so many of us at the front of the line. And here's the reasons why. And we know the reasons why. Oh my god, when we were hiring you [for *Hadestown*], it was like . . .

**Who is this guy? I seemingly dropped out of the sky.**

Wouldn't you expect people, especially in our business, to look at the résumé and call someone? It doesn't matter what color you are. It doesn't. It almost doesn't matter your qualifications. Because, really, it is about word of mouth.

**Exactly. And it's always been that way.**

I know that when I went in, I was called for this job by RCI. By David Richards, the president of the company. He called me. He's like, "hey," and I'm like, "hey!" He put me in front of Rachel [Chavkin], who didn't know me from a hole in the wall, but Rachel did her homework. She picked up the phone and she called several people on my résumé. That's what you're supposed to do. There's no shame in that. But it's the intent. Are you looking to see if this person is qualified? Or are you looking to say, "is this person a troublemaker?"

**In thinking about this role, how do you exist within a job description of what you do? How do you exist as the mom here, and what do you have to take care of?**

My normal line that I say of what a stage manager does, is that, once the creative team leaves, it is our job to uphold the integrity of the show. That's what we do. Now, what does Beverly Jenkins bring to it? There are people who are technically really strong, and I'm fine with technicals. I can call a cue or flip a button with the best of them. But what I like about my job is I'm a people person. And I understand that this job of theatre is really, really, really demanding. It asks a lot of people because people have to come in here and they have to tell a story every night. During the day, you don't know what they do with their life. We are transient people. It's all about what you're doing next. And it's hard, and people come in and they are bringing their lives in here. And I like that challenge. I like trying to make the building that you're coming into, where you're going to spend more time than with your real family, at least comfortable. I cannot always be successful. There are people who just like being miserable, and there are people who just love that. Nothing much I can do about that except try and meet them and be like, okay, so what are you miserable about today? Be miserable together.

**What are some specific ways in which you try and do that? Like, do you have any specific tricks?**

Come on, say it with me. Hand turkeys!

**Do we need to tell the people?**

Hand turkeys! You know, like when you're in first grade or Kindergarten and put your hand on a piece of construction paper.

**That's our tradition.**

Do the outline. It's a tradition and it's a competition. I love the things that have nothing to do with theatre, but make it fun. We just finished the door decorating contest. Mr. De Shields, of course, won again. I haven't been able to do it on this show, but something else that I like to do is "Who's Your Mama?" around Mother's Day. Everybody brings in a picture of their mom. Post it up. I don't have to say what decade, just a picture of your mom and then you have to guess who's whose mom. Who do you belong to? That's a fun time.

**You're very good at that here. Every theatre, I would argue in many ways, takes on the energy of the stage manager, and all of the team.**

The stage management office, like the kitchen in a Black home, is the heart of the building. And if that heart is diseased, the building is diseased. There's nothing you can do about it. I know other stage managers have this, but I love my open door policy. Come in, talk to me. You need to close the door, close the door. What's said behind that closed door really is between me and you. And if I need to tell it to someone else, I'm going to ask you: may I please share this with someone because this needs to be shared. So, there's a trust that I like to have with my company. It is not a given thing. It's an earned thing and I know it's earned.

**Do any of your experiences stand out to you?**

My favorite experience was *Miss Saigon*. Hands down. It taught me something about everything about how I am as a stage manager. I told you I have a stage management mom, and I also have my stage management dad. His name is Tom Capps. And so I'm a little bit of both in the way I handle myself. I learned what a theatre family is. Because there was nothing stronger than that bond. Than those people in that building. And it's not just about the cast; the theatre family is from the ushers, all the way to the back. I know that there's the ushers, the front of house, and the the folks in the back, but it doesn't mean you can't include them. And so I learned what a theatre family was, and I learned how to be sensitive to people's needs. I learned how to hear what people are saying, not just the words coming out of their mouth. What are you really saying.

**Do you think a lot about your legacy?**

I think that I am brown and I'm in this business. That is very exclusive.

**Was there ever a life before theatre for you?**

No. It was not a life before theatre. Theatre was always there. I went to school for theatre. Back in the olden days, the first performance memory I have was in my home. We had a bay window, and we used to perform. It looked like a little mini stage and we used to open up the traveler and perform for my mom and she'd sit there and just watch us, like lots of moms. But, she had a lot of us. And then I also remember my brother Michael, who was a musician, had a garage band and I was the Go-Go girl when I was six. And all I ever wanted was to have a bird cage like Goldie Hawn had. I wanted a cage. So I had my Go-Go boots with the white pattern leather with the zippers in the front. Thank you. And then, in elementary school, I was picked by my very, very, very progressive third grade teacher to be in a show. I remember singing at assembly. You go, you got your white shirt on, blue skirt, and I'm singing "The Star Spangled Banner" the way I heard it sang on television at the baseball games when opera people were singing it. So I was singing at the top of my belting lungs. That's how I was singing at seven, eight years old. And she was looking down at me like, what the hell? And so I got picked to be Anna in *The King and I.*

**So you were a stage person?**

I was always. There was never a question that I was not. Now, stage management is something I fell into. It was not what I ever thought I was going to do.

**What gave you the momentum to make the swap from being the performer on stage to helping other people do this?**

I went to college at Howard University. HU! Why did I go to Howard? A) I was accepted. B) Because Roberta Flack went there. And if it was good enough for her, it was good enough for me.

**That was the marker.**

If it's good enough for Roberta Flack, then it's good enough for me. I went to Howard as an actress. I also went there because I did not want to hear, especially while I was in college and I was paying people for education, that "we just couldn't put you in the part because you're Black." And that was not going to happen because that happened to me in junior high school. And I really appreciate my junior high school teacher being honest with me saying "the PTA will never go for it. They will never fund this show if I cast you and this other actor Jeffrey together. They will not go for it." That was in *Pyjama Game*.

**That's a really profound thing to let guide your selection at that age. The way that you were in complete control of your own destiny and said, "I am going to do this."**

Because I would be regulated to playing the friend. At best.

**And instead you're like, I can act. I can do this.**

I don't need to be the friend, I need to be *The*. So I went to Howard and it was one of the best decisions ever.

**And then stage management eventually.**

Well, it was pretty quick. What happened is I went to Howard. And, God rest his soul, Louis Johnson, who was a choreographer, for the spring show, was coming down to choreograph and direct *The Wiz*. Now, I had not taken a dance lesson since I was five years old. I come from a large family and we just didn't have the money, but I moved well. So I went to the dance audition, I sang, and then the cast list goes up, and you go look on the list. You see, Dorothy will be played by so-and-so. And that's all cool. I'm a freshman. And then you get down to the ensemble, you see all your friends, names and your name is not up there. "So I didn't know what the job os "assistant stage manager" was, but you know what? I was . . . like, okay. Okay, great. So I didn't know, but you know what? I was given something to do. And it's theatre, and it's my love. And I'm like, I'm doing it. Props? Word. I'm there. You want me to do it? I'll do it. I'm about that because I was learning. And so I went to my first production meeting. And that changed my life. Because in that production meeting, we talked about how the color of the backdrop affects the color of the costume affects the lighting instruments that will be used and with the effects, and we'll use this color and the stage bits here and this actress does this and all of that stuff. I'm like, oh, this is theatre. And that's where I learned what theatre was. And it also happened that in the Fall of my sophomore year that the College of Fine Arts was creating a new major, which was arts administration. And I was the first to sign up.

**Oh my god. That's legendary.**

So there you go. There's a need that you have to be a performer. And the need is I need to breathe. If it's anything less than that, don't bother. Because you will not survive. You will be angry and you'll just be doing it because it's something you do. But if you really love it, that is what you do. Period. You know? But management was my thing. And I enjoyed the parts that no one else saw. They just saw the results. And so if you don't see me but you see my work and it makes that person look fabulous, I have done a good job.

**Did you ever think that you would win a Tony?**

Absolutely not. Why would I?

**Yeah, of course.**

First off, Mr. De Shields has reminded me that *he* is a Tony winner. *I* am a Tony recipient.

**Oh, for heaven's sake. [*Laughs.*]**

**What would your hope be for the next generation? Does the landscape in terms of who's doing this type of work need to change much?**

The landscape is definitely changing. The landscape changed the second we shut down and the second we didn't come back four weeks later. The landscape changed. Landscapes changed when our friends started dying. And the most famous, of course, is our beloved Nick Cordero, when he passed away. His wife was so public with it. We thank her for sharing that, especially his Broadway family. The landscape changed when people like myself, who didn't have time before, found ourselves 24/7 caretakers of elderly parents all of a sudden. So the landscape changed. So to come back and say, "we work from eleven to midnight, six days a week", makes no sense. We can't continue living like that. It's too much to ask and expect from people. It's not something that will happen overnight, no matter how much every producer comes back and takes that pledge that we're going to do better. It's hard to do it immediately. But I do have faith that down the line, changes will be implemented to make it easier.

**Do you see more instances of that change?**

Yes. Yes, absolutely. I already see changes, even though it's still a work in progress. And it's happening everywhere. Stage managers. Actors on stage. Even the crews are changing. It was common in the past for crew jobs to be inherited. "My dad had this job, I have this job, and I'm passing it down to my son." That's how it was for decades. And now, that too is changing.

**I think our show here at *Hadestown* is a perfect example.**

It is, because from the top, the thought is put into it. And it has to be, especially for white people who are not used to being around others. You have to think about it. And no matter how open and progressive and liberal you think you are, you *think* you are, you still have to work at it.

**There's so much learning still to be done.**

Walking in the *Hadestown* building with all the different colors and races and nationalities, it's easy to have conversation with people. It's not like, "oh, I have to not say this." It's easy to have conversation. And I don't have to put so much thought into it.

**That's one of the things I've always loved about working here is that it's a great representation of not only what should be on the stage, but eventually, one day what I think ideally, our audiences will look like. I think that's probably one of the final hurdles.**

Absolutely.

**How is the work of Broadway & Beyond going now that we've reopened?**

It's going swimmingly. We have eleven stage managers on Broadway right now, who came through and who got hired from going through our meet and greet session.

**That's the evidence, right?**

I have been actively trying to hire someone to come in for a while here at *Hadestown*. And everyone I'm calling is like, "oh I'm busy. I'm busy." And that is music to my ears. I hate it because I'm the one who needs somebody, but it's music to my ears that we have had any part in this. And it didn't take much. It's not like we had to beg people to participate. The first time we had it, we had to pick up the phone, write emails, call friends. And, because everybody was home, it was easy to do it. And people from all over the country could meet people with Zoom. So it was wonderful. At first, we just had Broadway regional tours. With our last event we had a few weeks ago back in January, organizations came in to meet with stage managers. Cruise lines, opera, regional. It's major.

**Right. Because it's not just about what happens here in one part of the country. You've got to be thinking about this everywhere.**

We've got lots of people who are out on tours now, which is great. I know it's hard to believe, but not everybody's dream is to be on the Broadway. Sometimes it's like, "you know what, I like where I live in Chicago, I'd like to work here. I like where I live in San Diego. I like being on the road." Those road dogs love it.

**What are your hopes for the rest of your career?**

I think there are a few things. I want to go run the College of Fine Arts at Howard University.

**You hear this, students?**

I want to go run it.

**That's legacy right there on all sides of it. Alumnus, faculty.**

I also want to go work at the Rock and Roll Hall of Fame in Cleveland, Ohio. If anybody knows me, 100percent, I love pop music. 80s pop. And I also love pop history. I love it.

**I've always been able to tell because one of my favorite things about working with you has always been that you sing everything.**

I am a jukebox.

**You would sing every line in the show. And there's something to knowing your show well enough but also being brave in a room full of actors and singing. That is one thing I noticed instantly. You are a team collaborator and that's what this is. It's all collaboration.**

Look, I was a performer. There's still a little performer love in me. I don't need to do it. But, I like to joke with them, "Don't get twisted, I'll put that green (Persephone) dress on in a minute!" I like to say stuff like that. But in the rehearsal room, if it needs to be sung or somebody needs me to step in and do the two step or whatever, I can still do the two step. I don't care if my singing isn't good enough. It makes me happy. And I don't think I'm the worst singer out there.

**Far from it!**

I can hold a note. I know where it's supposed to be. If someone's missing, I'll sing all the parts on that, you know. But I'm also aware that I'm the stage manager. So you have to be careful, especially when you're singing the parts or that you are not trying to upstage, you're not auditioning: you're helping. If it needs to be filled in, I can sing it, but I'm not auditioning. Now, there are times at understudy rehearsal where I will perform for the masses, because it's fun. But there's a difference.

**Is there anything that you want future stage managers of the world or anyone in the theatre who's picking this up, especially young people, to know?**

I think when I drive. I also sing when I drive. Me and David Bowie.

**You must be, one would say, maybe deeply, deeply obsessed with Bowie.**

David Bowie was everything. He was, is, everything.

**I'm a huge Bowie fan too!**

He's almost like the Bible. If you're going through something, you can find something in the Bible. If you're going through something and you need something, you can find it in his life or in his music. He's everything. And he was honest about it. But you asked me about anything the young readers should know. The thing that I keep coming back to is three words: never be less. Never be less than who you are. Never be less than what you want to be. Never be less. Period. Don't let someone steer you into being less. Don't let someone tell you you're less because they're really projecting onto you. They're less because they just want to make sure that they feel they're better. Just never be less. That's it.

**What a hard thing to affirm especially when we're younger, right? We all go through that, even at different phases in our career, where you feel more empowered or less empowered.**

Now, "never be less" does not mean, if you are asked to do something, to ever think it's below you because you never know who's looking. I'll tell one story. I always like to tell my pencil story. Because this is a "never be less" story. I was already established as a stage manager. I had already PSM-ed several shows. And I was between my own gigs, so I went over to *Aida* and I was subbing. Clifford Schwartz (hey Cliffy!) was the production supervisor and he was in because the PSM was on vacation. We had never worked together, but we got on just royally. So one day I'm in the office, he's in the office and he's writing and he says, "Beverly, I know you're a real stage manager." And I'm like, "yeah." And he says, "Can you do me a favor? Can you please sharpen my pencils?" And I said, "oh my god, of course." I took his pencils and sharpened them. Do you know the next time Clifford had to ask me to sharpen his pencils? Never. Because I understood that if he's asking me to sharpen his pencils, this is a tool that he needs. He needs it sharpened so he can do his job. And so he never, ever had to ask again for sharpened pencils because I made it my job each day to come in, top of day, and sharpen his pencils. How easy is that? But you know who else noticed that he had sharpened pencils? Clifford Schwartz. So, you know how many times Clifford Schwartz has called me for a job? Many.

**It's as simple as that. You never know.**

You never know. It doesn't make you less because someone asks you, can you please help me keep my tools sharpened? If you were the nurse in the operating room and the doctor says, "Can you hand me a scalpel?", you would have to have it ready. That's basically what he's asking me to do for him. Make sure that his stuff is there. It's a simple thing. And it kept me employed. Everybody has their own experience.

And when it all comes back to it, being that person of color is different. I was on a Zoom just yesterday. Thirty-something people and I was like, "There's me. And oh, there's the only other person of color." And it's 2022. We still got a long way to go.

# LINDA TWINE

**Linda Twine's** career as a music director and conductor on Broadway and across the US is legendary—she is a trailblazing Black artist. Her first Broadway role was as a substitute musician in the pit band for *The Wiz*, before going on to be at the helm of many important Black productions and a variety of Broadway musicals. Twine's work in building the sound of groundbreaking musicals has shaped pit bands, as has her dedication to mentoring and creating opportunities for musicians to follow in her footsteps.

She was born in 1945 in Muskogee, Oklahoma, and was inducted into her home state's Hall of Fame in 2007. She graduated from Oklahoma City University before studying at Manhattan School of Music and moving to New York. She worked in public schools in the day, while in the evening working with church choir and professional theatre productions. Her career on Broadway includes working as music director and conductor for *The Color Purple*, *Caroline or Change*, *A Year with Frog and Toad*, *Jelly's Last Jam*, and *Big River*. She was also associate conductor and pianist for *The Wild Party*. Lena Horne selected Twine to be her conductor for her fifteen-part band for her biographical show: *Lena Horne: The Lady and her Music*. She worked on *The Color Purple* from its early development and pre-Broadway production in Atlanta, Georgia in 2004 onto Broadway in 2005.

Twine has composed and arranged theatrical works for Off-Broadway theatre, regionally and internationally. She has published a range of choral works, including collections for the Boys Choir of Harlem, the Harlem Spiritual Ensemble, and the cantata "Changed My Name"—inspired by Sojourner Truth and Harriet Tubman. Throughout her career, Twine has been committed to music education and community building. She has mentored many Broadway professionals including Joseph Joubert (who worked with her as conductor-sub on *Big River*, and as orchestrator on *The Color Purple*); and Jeanine Tesori.

**How was music part of your home life?**

There was always a piano in the house: it was my grandmother's piano. My uncle says that she read music, and she liked to play piano. Back in the day people would just come by, knock on your door, and sell you music. If you had a piano, they'd sit down and play it. My father also played piano, even though he was a lawyer. And he loved Fats Waller's music. And I think while we lived in my grandmother's house he probably played a lot of Fats Waller's music every day of my life.

**At what point did you know "I'm going to be a musician one day"?**

Well, when I was a kid, most of the kids, most of the other children, including me, took piano lessons. And so on Saturdays, that's where you, that's where you went for at least an hour. My mother found a wonderful teacher, Eleanor Barwell. I took two lessons a week. Whenever there was a contest or competitions, I would come every day. And she would say you don't have to pay for these extra lessons, she'd say, "I just want you to be prepared." She had between four and six recitals a year we had to participate in. I had an excellent teacher. God assigned my mother finding *that* teacher to teach Linda in little old bitty Muskogee, Oklahoma.

**When did you decide you were going to study music at college?**

My mother decided that! I went to Oklahoma City University (OCU) and then, when I finished my four years, I was a piano major of all things. What does a Black person do with a piano major ... what is that, you know? To this day I don't regret it, and I didn't regret it then. But it made me go on to continue school as I still didn't know what I was going to do.

My piano teacher at OCU was Nancy Apgar, and she was from Philadelphia and went to Eastman School of Music, and she thought I should go to New York to go to school. So, I went to Manhattan School [of Music] and then when I got out of there, I started teaching in a public school, Lord have mercy! PS113, and it was in the news everyday. I didn't know that, [*laughing*] in the 5 o'clock news!

There was this one first grade class that had six teachers already; the school had just been in session for two months. But I had a fantastic principal who loved music, and she thought it was very important that all the kids have music. They had a music teacher from Grade 3 through 5, and Fran Dorsey (another friend of mine who was an actress and a singer) took up half a week, and I took up half a week to fill a full time position. We had to do an assembly program once a month. So that was right up my alley—getting all the children [to sing]. Alright now, you've got me cooking!

**So you were prepping shows even then! Who inspired you who was working on Broadway?**

Joyce Brown was an incredible musician, conductor, orchestrator, composer. Joyce Brown was the conductor for *Purlie*, and that was the first Broadway show I'd seen on Broadway. I thought it was so fantastic, and the music was just poppin'—I said, oh my gosh, I would love to do something like this. I saw that show five times! The band always sounded fabulous—that was Joyce Brown. The "Exit Music"—that means the people are exiting and you are playing music while they exit—well, instead of people leaving, they gathered around the pit. Because Joyce Brown was conducting and the music just sounded great, and in that pit she had a majority Black pit.

**So what was the moment you said I'm going to start working in theatre?**

Well, two things: one is from the Studio where I lived and met my friend Gardenia Cole, she was an actress. Back in the day, Juilliard, Manhattan School, ran a school of music, none of these places had dormitories, so when you send your kid out of state—where are they gonna stay? They go to New York City . . . have to get an apartment? So there was a place called the Studio Club, which was a Y[WCA], but a long term residence for students and for women just to live who were working.

Gardenia was an actress, coming from South Carolina, and she was a student at the Afro American Studio, and they were doing a production of James Baldwin's *Amen Corner*, and they needed a pianist. She told the director, oh I know somebody! That was me! That is exactly where it began. I know somebody, I played for the three performers, and then Joe ??? [*line drops*] Joe Papp [*line drops for longer*] a pianist, and would you be interested and of course I had no job or nothing.

And I said, well yes. And I went and met her, and we worked together for about fifteen years. But I learned so much just from that gig.

But that's where it started, him seeing me at the *Amen Corner* at the Afro-American studio. He recommended me to Novella Nelson, so I played for her gigs. I was teaching PS113, that school that was in the news everyday, and working for Novella at night, at Reno Sweeney's, which was a very upscale cabaret place.

Michelle [Cheryl] Hardwicke was the young lady who had the keyboard chair in *The Wiz*. She saw me, and she was looking for a woman to be her sub. She came up to me after one set and asked me, would I like to be her sub. And that's the train, right there. You know that's luck right? You know that? Are you aware of that? And the Lord is walking with me too.

**Well there you go, it can't just be luck you know. Someone saw you and said, this is clearly the path you were meant for!**

Well, my first inclination was to say no, no no, I can't do this, but I made myself say yes. But the music supervisor of *The Wiz* was also the music supervisor of *Ain't Misbehavin'*. So when the show stopped, they were getting ready to do a London company, a National company, and a bus and truck tour. And they thought it was a good idea to train all the companies at one time, and they found out later that does not work. It's too many . . .! But, they asked me to do rehearsals, and I said yes; I was very familiar with Fats Waller's music anyway because of my father.

After the rehearsals were over, they put me with the Broadway company to cover Hank Jones, the pianist on stage. They said, you just come to the show twice a week, give notes. And then, on rehearsal day, you know, see if you can correct some of these things; but do you know I came everyday just to hear Hank Jones play, you know. Just to hear him play and just idolize what he was doing. It was just a treat every night because that big old band was on stage and I had the best seat in the house.

**Hank Jones was a massive player on the Broadway scene at the time.**

With *Ain't Misbehavin'* Luther Henderson handpicked him. Henderson was the orchestrator of *Ain't*. And he handpicked the band. So when I went on, when I started going on when Hank would take off, these guys, I said Lord, look who's in this band here! And little old me!

**And where did you go from *Ain't Misbehavin'*?**

Arthur Faria was the choreographer for *Ain't Misbehavin'*. He was the director for Lena's upcoming show. He called me and said I knew I had covered *Ain't*, which was still running. You have to take chances on these shows because you don't know if they're gonna run or not. It was rumoured that *Ain't* was gonna close in two months, and they had this big blockbuster coming in, starring Chita Rivera and Donald O'Connor, you know, from *Singin' in the Rain*. It was supposed to be the next big hit. So I jumped ship, and went to that show, called *Bring Back Birdie*. It opened on Thursday and closed on Saturday. And *Ain't* ran another year!

So Arthur calls me and says, "Linda? Would you like to play rehearsals and play second chair on Lena Horne's show, and it's gonna run five weeks." That's what it was scheduled to run. And I said yes, I'd do that. And lo and behold I got elevated.

**What was it like working for Lena Horne, one of the legends of our time?**

Well, we were onstage, and she introduced me not only as Linda Twine, so you get my name, but as her daughter: "Ladies and Gentlemen, I want to introduce you to . . . my daughter Linda Twine." I didn't really appreciate it at the time because I'm thinking ahead, what's the next tempo, what's the tempo! [*Laughter.*] You're always thinking ahead.

**I'm struck by that image of a Black woman as the conductor, as the leader of the show. I'm curious, did you ever consider yourself a role model for younger Women of Color, especially at a time when there weren't many Black women conducting?**

No. None of that occurred to me *at all* until it's over. While I was in the moment I was just trying to keep up and do a good job for that night, you know. But, the reception, the reception of seeing a *woman* up there, you know that really startled me. But it was like, they're used to seeing horses and I was a zebra.

One time I was walking down in San Francisco, and I caught a newspaper in a street container. And I said, wait a minute, this picture looks familiar. There's my picture! It was like that in every city. And I'd send them home to my folks, and they'd be like what is this?!

**Folks back home in Oklahoma must have followed your career with tremendous interest.**

I was out passing through the subway coming through 42nd Street one time, and noticed numerous TV cameras there, but I went on about my way. Somebody from Muskogee called me and said, "I saw you on TV going through the subway!" I always had a lot of support from my church as well.

**I want to chat about that, because your church work has become such an important staple for the Black community on Broadway as well. That was something you always did in conjunction with your work on Broadway, so a lot of folks on Broadway had spent time at your church as well.**

Well, one of my friends who had been in *Amen Corner* had a father who was a minister, and so she was used to going to church a lot. Since I played for the Gospel Choir church where my father attended, and played on the organ at the Lutheran church every Sunday, I was just used going to church, and so I was looking for a church home.

I started going to St James because a friend of mine was singing in the choir, and the pulling point for me was that church started at 11:00 and they were out at 12:00! And at one point, the Choir Directorship opened up and they asked me to do that, so that's how I started with the choir up there.

**And the rest of the Broadway followed!**

I started doing a little fundraiser.

**The production every year!**

Yes, the production every year, and little stuff like that really caught on. So, I enjoyed all of that.

**So tell me—you've been involved with so many productions, and they've become big staples of our art. How do you feel about your role as a music director and conductor of so many productions, which inevitably you've left a huge fingerprint on as an artist. These have shaped what musical theatre is today. How do you feel on all that?**

Well, I never thought that I left a fingerprint on the music, although your job as music director or conductor is to interpret what the composers want, and to implement the director's direction. And so if I've done that, I didn't do it by myself; the cast was part of that also. It mutates. And what it finally looks like on opening night is because of those previews and those prior workshops.

**Did you have a favorite part of that process? Did you enjoy the workshops more? What was your favourite?**

I did. The first shows I was doing were shows that had already gone through their process and they were already set. I said, "Oh, I want to do a new show! I'd like to see what that is." Then after that, I said "Well, no, I'd take an old show!" You need to work! New shows are thrilling because it's the creation of it. You can see that we have come from Point A to Point G.

**Were there any shows that you did the workshops for that stand out for you?**

I really enjoyed *The Color Purple* workshops. They were special.

**Tell us a bit about that journey with that too. I'm sure that must be one of those moments that you look back upon on your career and say "wow"!**

Well, even before that, I think about *Big River*, for instance. I enjoyed Roger Miller being around for that. It'd just be so thrilling. And Roger Miller's from Oklahoma; how's that for a connection that helped me through my journey!

And Lena [Horne]'s show [*Lena Horne: The Lady and Her Music*] was like that too. She was doing all standards, but the way she would interpret all those lyrics! That was my coming of age for understanding lyrics. She was the master at that. Every person in the house thought she was talking to them. Just one on one communication. You can do that, you've got something.

**You've worked with so many people . . . Eartha Kitt too!**

Oh, she'd have *loved* you! [*Laughing.*] She was a delightful person, and the history she *lived* through. Good god Almighty. We were in rehearsal once, and everybody's in this eight-hour call, and you have one hour or two hours. Eartha is doing exercises in the corner, and she had a real tricky number in that show [*The Wild Party*] that changed metre in every bar. So, I said to her, "Eartha, just watch me, I'm gonna bring you in." She appreciated that! I loved her, and grew up idolizing her.

**Let's go back to *Color Purple* for a moment. What was that like?!**

Well, introducing yourself to Alice Walker's work is something itself. These composers took it and ran with it. We did a workshop with three weeks of performances. A workshop in Atlanta. There were some songs that didn't even make it into New York that I loved, because they had a tone of music that reflected the setting. You didn't even have to hear *what* the performers were saying; you knew you were there right at the turn of the century.

**That's incredible. Just legendary musicians too! Brenda Russell . . .**

Oh, she'd sit down and play a new tune . . . as I look back, it was amazing.

**Allee Willis. Lots of theatre and pop music crossover artists with huge influence.**

Just meeting those folks was just amazing. But they wanted that music *exactly* like they wrote it. And they wrote in *all* of the riffs, so you didn't need to put in riffs, unless you really knew how to.

**That's amazing, and all of that is part of that process. By the time I saw that score, we know exactly what they wanted because it tells you every note. You get that even in the orchestration of it, with what [Joseph] Joubert had done. It's incredible seeing that specificity and knowing that you were right there in the room as that was happening.**

Absolutely. The vocal work of the second [the revival] *Color Purple* was good. The music was really good.

**It was such a different production in its reconceptualization. It must have been quite the experience for you to walk in and see something that was part of your DNA, and yet was so different. You must have been such a support to the company. People don't think about this, but the conductor is always the person who they spend the most time in front of every single performance. You're always there with them.**

Yeah, I was like Mama. I went through rehearsals with another Black stage manager in Chicago and, as two Black women, we were running a tight ship. I'm telling you, all the kids understood the rules!

**How do we make this journey into theatre an easier one for women of color? Do you think it has shifted since you started do you think, and where do you think we have to go?**

Well—there are more opportunities for people of color than when I started. Joyce Brown was one of the first women conductors [of color]. I once said I think I'll always be doing Black shows. It just works out like that. We had a large Black ensemble in Big River. But we mustn't limit ourselves to only Black works as Black artists. I mean, look at Joseph Joubert's résumé; that's scary! Go on boy! [*Laughing.*] Amazing. He's a conductor, orchestrator, arranger. He's just amazing. Just a sweetheart, just a very giving person. Just like you!

**We call you Miss Twine for a reason! You are a role model and a mentor for so many of us.**

I wish I'd done more!

**I'd argue that you've done so much more than I think you even give yourself credit for! Those of us in the business who are still doing it so actively are all so lucky to have you as Mama!**

**You've now earned the time to be able to step back and take a bit of a slower pace of things! Do you have any hope for new works?**

Definitely! We've been in this pandemic for so long, but we can get out of it if we get our vaccinations and stay masked.

**Staying healthy, even post-pandemic, is vital for our industry. It will reflect how healthy we can be as we can do the work.**

We have to support each other and pass the word on.

**For our readers—you've mentioned Joyce Brown a couple of times, and it's important for our readers to know who she was. As a conductor, she did a lot of work—she conducted shows like *Purlie* back in the 1970s, but we've been having tons of conversations around equitable access in the theatre even today. Are we right in believing that was something that was on her mind even fifty years ago?**

Oh I bet so! Joyce Brown was an incredible musician, conductor, orchestrator, composer. She is often credited with being the first Black conductor on Broadway. She was the conductor for *Purlie*, and that was the first Broadway show I'd seen on Broadway. A friend of mine said to me, "You have to go!" The first time I'd seen it was in previews. I thought it was so fantastic, and the music was just poppin'!

I knew I would love to do something like this, either as a conductor or in the pit. I saw that show five times, and every time people came to town, I said let's go see *Purlie*. The band always sounded fabulous—and that was Joyce Brown. People gathered around the pit for the Exit Music. But she was very nice, and very, very motherly.

**Very much like you!**

She was very supportive—always encouraging us Black artists to keep pushing on. But the shows were few and far between for Black folk. She had a majority Black pit. Luther Henderson had done some of the dance arrangements, which were incredible. That was my favourite show for a long time.

I came to visit Melba Moore, who was wonderful. But my favourite was Sherman Hemsley—he was incredible! I just fell in love with those actors.

Some of these names you're throwing down! To think of seeing him on stage ... And it speaks so much to everything you've said: how important community is within the Black Broadway network. There is Broadway as a community, but we've had to find solidarity as Black members of Broadway as well. You've been such a pillar of Black Broadway for so long. It's pretty remarkable.

There was one show I did—I'm not going to name it—but they hired me as the conductor, and they were hiring the band. I just had to really holler and say, "I'm not going to be the only Black person in this band!"

That's incredible though, because those are the conversations we're still having today, and you are saying that was happening even so many years back. That's an incredible reminder for all of us—to keep on pushing as the song says. The fact that you were advocating for that is inspiration for us these days.

I have to be able to look out for the young women too. Even just to come see the pit of *Color Purple*—there were two. Two! So you ask, where do you find them? I think we have to go to the music schools and ask, where are those conductors? Who is studying conducting?

Yes, absolutely! We're as close to it as we've ever been and that doesn't mean we don't a long way to go still. But thanks to so many, including you as like one of the trailblazers of all this, you're will always be somebody that all of us think of.

Your remarkable career as a Broadway conductor is truly one of the most legendary that the Broadway community has ever known, period. Period. And the fact that as a Black woman that you've done what you have done despite difficulties in our industry is remarkable.

Thank you. And here's to the next generation of conductors!

# STAFFORD ARIMA

 **Stafford Arima** is currently the Artistic Director of the largest regional theatre in Southern Alberta, Canada: Theatre Calgary. Arima was nominated for an Olivier Award for his direction of the West End premiere of *Ragtime*; and in 2015 he became the first Asian Canadian to direct a musical (*Allegiance*) on Broadway. Additional Broadway credits include *Seussical* (Associate Director) and *A Class Act* (Associate Director). He directed the world premiere productions of *Bhangin' It* (La Jolla Playhouse), *Altar Boyz* (Off-Broadway), *Dial M For Murder* (The Old Globe, CA), *Ace* (Cincinnati Playhouse), *Two Class Acts: Ajax & Squash* (The Flea Theatre, NYC), *The New World* (Bucks County Playhouse), *The Tin Pan Alley Rag* (Roundabout Theatre Company), *Poster Boy* (Williamstown Theatre Festival), *Mary and Max—A New Musical* (Theatre Calgary), and *Forgiveness* (The Arts Club, Vancouver). Additional credits include *Carrie* (MCC Theatre, Off-Broadway), *bare* (Off-Broadway revival), *The Secret Garden—In Concert* (Lincoln Center), *Jacques Brel Is Alive and Well and Living In Paris* (Stratford Festival), and *A Christmas Carol* and *Billy Elliot* (Theatre Calgary). Arima is a graduate of York University (Canada), and a former adjunct and Granada Artist in Residence at the University of California, Davis. He is a founding Board member of the Canadian Guild of Stage Directors and Choreographers, and a proud member of CAEA and SDC. Website: staffordarima.com

**What was the moment you knew theatre was
what you wanted to do for life?**

I was eleven years old. My mother and I were on Spring Break, and she
took me to Los Angeles. It was a week-long excursion and I was so excited.
eleven years old, going to see Universal Studios and SeaWorld and Disney
Land, all of that stuff. But my mother loved the theatre. And she loved
musicals. So, she took me on a matinee to see *Evita* at the Shubert Theatre,
which is no longer in existence. I was really upset because it was a matinee
so it was in the afternoon and I didn't know why we were going. We were
sitting in the last row of the last balcony. It was 1980, and it was the
*Hamilton* of that time—it was the popular show. Loni Ackerman was Eva
Perón. I sat there sulking in the seat and I didn't know anything about Eva
Perón or *Evita* or Andrew Lloyd Webber or Harold Prince. But then the
lights dimmed.

What I really remember is that it looked like little ants running around
this stage, and that is where I was bitten by the theatre bug. So, it
manifested for me. I became an *Evita* diehard fan and I had to get the
record—the double fold one with Patti and Mandy and all of the original
Broadway cast. From that point on, I loved *Evita* and I loved theatre. I've
seen *Evita* probably over fifty times now. I would see it anywhere. When
my mother took me to New York for the first time, *Evita* was definitely on
the list. When she took me to the West End for the first time, we saw it. I
saw the touring productions. I saw the dinner theatre production at Stage
West in Mississauga (outside of Toronto). It didn't matter to me, as long
as it was *Evita*. That's really where I think I discovered my love for
musicals, and specifically for the genre of going into a darkened room
with a lot of other people and experiencing that live energy. That
manifested into a desire to then become a performer. That led to,
inevitably, directing. Although it wasn't a natural switch, I would say *Evita*
was really the catalyst for my interest and passion in this world we call the
theatre.

**What I love most about that story is, from that moment in
Los Angeles onward, you had planted the seed for yourself
that would end up nurturing the existence of your work in
New York and on the West End and in Canada. I think that's the
biggest lesson for all of us as theatre practitioners—that good theatre
is everywhere.**

It is, it really is. I've had a real fortunate experience to be able to witness theatre on all levels. I say to any emerging artist or young student that the best piece of advice I can give is to see everything. Everything. It could be a fringe show, it could be a Broadway show, it could be an amateur production, it could be a community theatre production, it could be a touring production. Go and see theatre everywhere. And that was my greatest education, even though I didn't know it at the time. Prior to musical theatre exploding in the mid-90s, I went to everything in Toronto, from Buddies in Bad Times to Tarragon to the Royal Alex touring shows or the Broadway series that would come through the O'Keefe Centre. I had three filing drawers of these programmes I'd keep. I didn't keep them all which is the unfortunate thing when you start purging as you grow older. Some of the more sentimental things I kept. But yes, witnessing is the greatest education one can get, even if you don't know what you're looking for. You start to, in a subtle way, build your taste. What do you connect with? It could be anything. It could be a style of theatre. Mine was in Los Angeles, California. My first inaugural experience.

**From there, how did your journey as a performer start?**

I really didn't start any kind of theatre studies until high school. I went to Newtonbrook Secondary High in North York (Toronto). It was there that I really found an outlet. I was taking theatre. It was called "theatre" with Dene Lettman and Carol Welton, and I participated in the high school shows.

**It's amazing you even remember the names. I think that's a common thing in all of these interviews is that we absolutely remember the names of the people who set us on that path. We all know who those people are.**

Absolutely! Dene and Carol. They co-taught theatre and did the high school musicals. My first one was *Guys and Dolls*, where I played Lieutenant Brannigan. The next one I did was *Damn Yankees*, and the third was *Little Shop of Horrors*. I was never singing solo, because I wasn't a singer. But it's funny, I think about *Guys and Dolls*. I obviously wanted a part. I wanted to be in the show and we had to audition. Dene Lettman was the director. I guess in many ways this was the beginning of the director in me, although I didn't know it. I thought to myself, and I shared with her, that you should hire me as Lieutenant Brannigan. She asked "why" and I said, "Well, because actually it would be quite funny." She said, what do you mean? And I said, "Well, look at me. What do you see?" And she said, "Stafford." I said, "No, no, what do you see?" And she didn't really want to say it. So I said, "well, I'm Asian". Lieutenant Brannigan is an Irish cop with a very thick Irish brogue. So there's something funny about an Asian person walking out and speaking with a thick Irish brogue. And she cast me. When I came out and said my first line, it was with a thick Irish brogue. Well, the audience burst out laughing. An Asian person speaking with a thick Irish brogue. And of course, I didn't know it back then, but that probably was a little bit of the director in me looking at a bigger picture versus just an actor. I can remember I was always a little bit more comfortable when we would do group projects in class. And Dene would say, "We're doing a docudrama on a word, so pick the word." And our word was nakedness. And then she said, "Okay, figure out who your team is." I always picked the director role. Even though I didn't know that directing was going to be in my future, it obviously was lurking around there on some level.

**You went to York (University) and did some postsecondary work?**

Yes. From Newtonbrook, I then auditioned for the York University Theatre program. I didn't want to go to York. I really wanted to go to Ryerson because I wanted to be an actor. I didn't need a university degree and so wanted to go to Ryerson or maybe the National Theatre School. My mother basically said, "you have to get a degree." And at that point, Ryerson wasn't giving a degree. She said, "I don't care if you get a degree in basket weaving. You have to get a degree, get that piece of paper." And I fought her on that because I didn't want a degree. I wanted much more isolated training. But she forced me and she said, quotations. I got a scholarship to York for the first year. It's funny how prescient all of this was because, when I was going for my green card, the first thing on the top of the application was, do you have a university degree? I had to have a university degree in order for me to get my green card. She didn't know that I was going to move to the States but, in some mystical way, forcing me to go to university, inevitably, was the best thing for me. At York, Ron Singer, who was a professor there, was really instrumental in awakening the idea that there was a director in me. And so I really have Ron to thank for opening that possibility. I graduated with a Theatre Studies degree. I didn't go into the acting stream, nor the directing stream, nor the design stream. I went into the theatre study stream, which basically allowed you to take courses in all of the areas versus just acting. So I was able to take acting classes, design classes, dance classes, and then I did what I considered a minor in psychology. I really felt that it was important for me as a director: to understand how the mind works. We think about acting, we think about characters, what's their intention? Why are they the way they are?

**What a tremendous thing for our readers who might be considering a career in directing to consider. One of the biggest things a mentor told me once was, don't get caught up in the world of theatre. Keeping all of your plates full with understanding of how the world works will make you the best theatre practitioner you can be. It's understanding people, which is what you do as a director.**

I didn't really have any mentors. No one in my family worked in the theatre. No one worked in the arts field. I guess my mentor was Ron Singer. But he was just giving me focus, direction, and awakenings towards directing. My first mentor really was Hal Prince even though I didn't go to a class with him. I assisted him on *Show Boat*. So, just being in that room with him was really kind of a mentorship. During York, I worked at Live Entertainment (Livent), which was Garth Drabinsky's company. I was the receptionist. I answered an ad in the *Toronto Star* that was looking for a receptionist for a large entertainment company. I remember talking to my mother about it and I said, should I? And she said, no, don't apply there. She said, apply smaller. Go to Tarragon. But I wanted to work for the big company. I didn't know it was Garth's company and I didn't know it was Livent but I applied. And I remember Jen Swenson, who was the office manager at Livent from New York. Real thick New York accent. And she said, do you know how to use a Meridian SL1 switchboard? And this was the old days, right? And I said yes. She said, okay, how? And I lied. I made up a story. I didn't know how to use an SL1 Meridian switchboard. Anyway, she hired me. I came in on Monday, petrified. Thank goodness, there was a manual to the left of the switchboard. I read the thing, I called my friends and said, call this number. And they called the number so the thing would light up. I literally learned how to use this thing at 8am. Then my time at Livent went from being the receptionist to then becoming the Secretary to the Executive Vice President. Then I became the fill-in Secretary to Garth Drabinsky. I was then moved into the Press Department where I became the Press Assistant. I didn't realize at that time all of the nutrients that I was receiving, from Receptionist to Executive Assistant, to answering phone calls for Garth, hearing and reading contracts that were coming through, or seeing how correspondence happened between producer and director.

**That's the best training you could have ever asked for.**

I was soaking it all in. It was in many ways my Masters' degree in theatre producing. I didn't go get another degree. I just sunk myself into an environment where I could learn. Ten years after graduating in 1992, I didn't direct anything for ten years: I assisted (directed), I was a resident director, but I never directed anything of my own. Until *Altar Boyz* in New York. *Altar Boyz* was the first, really, and that didn't really happen until it opened Off-Broadway. So, for ten years, I was still going to school. Even though I wasn't in an institution: I was in an institution of practical theatre. And through Livent, I worked as a casting associate at Johnson-Liff Casting, which is long gone now, but they were the original casting directors of *Phantom, Les Mis, Miss Saigon, Joseph*.

**I love that you're a lifelong learner, but you've also embraced that moment we've all had when we were starting up and wanting to do something, while doing all of these things we didn't want to do. You don't realize how much all of these things along the way feed you to getting there. It's all part of creating you as the unique artist which nobody talks about. How all of your individual skills and experiences ultimately do feed what you're able to do.**

It also unconsciously gave me an awareness of other things. So, if I had to, I could probably have become a publicist because I had some experience at Livent. I could have parlayed that into working for Boneau/Bryan-Brown or somebody in the States, or whatever I was going to do. Or be an administrator. I'm fifty-two years old (fifty-four as of 2023) so I may be a little old-school, but there is a part of me that still believes that one needs to focus. Someone says, I want to be a writer or a director or an actor. That's great. And you or whoever, probably have all of those skills to act, to sing, to write, to produce. But, in the early stages when we're fledgling little artists and we're trying to find our way in this world, I think that even though I didn't focus on directing, what I did focus on is musical theatre. I definitely surrounded myself with the idea that I wanted to work at the big entertainment firm, which inevitably became Broadway. Even though I was doing casting, press, assisting, secretary, receptionist, it was all in this commercial theatre world.

The other thing that I think is always important is when we have an Oprah "aha" moment. And to be aware of those moments. I wanted to be an actor. I was cast in a show at Tarragon Second Space. It was a play called *The Long and the Short and the Tall* by a British writer, Willis Hall, and I was cast in one of the leads. I was still in high school. I played a Japanese prisoner of war. It was basically a story about the friendship that forms between the British soldier and me, and how we're really alike. We both like chocolate, we both smoke, we both have girlfriends but, at the end of the play, he has to kill me. And the last scene is he shoots me in the head and I die, which is the casualty of war even though we're actually the same. There was a scene before the act break where we had a fight. It was choreographed, and he would pull on my shirt and we'd go one way and then the other way. This one performance, he pulled my shirt and all the buttons popped open. What was exposed was Stafford's fatty stomach. I didn't have six pack abs. I've never had six-pack abs. I was thinner than I am today, but I was still not in shape. And I remember we had the fight, and my belly was exposed. And then, the next moment, I'm supposed to sit on a crate. But that's not a good position to be in if you don't want your belly to show. So I remember trying to close my shirt. I got off at intermission and I literally had the *aha* moment.

What I realized at that moment was that I was not going to be the actor that I wanted to be. Not that I *couldn't* act, but that the actors I admired were those that gained 400 pounds for the role or lost 400 pounds for a role. I was instantly concerned about what was there under my shirt. That didn't mean that I woke up at intermission and said, I want to be a director, but something changed in, me. And if one isn't aware of those kinds of moments, those are moments to not forget. And that didn't mean that I thought it was bad, ugly, fat. It wasn't a self deprecating thought of "I'm a terrible person because my body is out of shape". It was, "if I really was the actor that I wanted to be, I would have got my body into shape for that role, because a soldier is not going to have a muffin top." Some awakenings that are so important for us as we traverse through this minefield of career.

**We don't talk about that a lot. Thinking about who you truly are as an artist. How you truly find your full self. It's that realization not out of, I can't do this, or this is bad, but just that this is clearly where I'm meant to be.**

Yeah. You know, the universe, She works in such extraordinary ways. She presents things to us that we don't necessarily want to see all the time. So you stay fluid. It doesn't mean losing your focus. I never wanted to be an artistic director. That wasn't even in my periphery at all. But a headhunter knocked on my door and asked me if I'd be interested. And I said, no. I wasn't interested. And then, only later, I took my own advice and thought, okay, wait, something's out there. Let's see what happens. And I was forty-seven. I made that kind of change that late in my life, moving into my fifties. But, again, it's still staying open to that ebb and flow of what comes our way.

**The hope for this book is that it really becomes something that theatre students can open at nineteen or twenty and say, how cool is this that this is written by somebody who actually looks like me or might be closer to looking like me than anyone else I've ever been in a room with.**

I remember, Kelly Nestruck wrote an article in *The Globe and Mail* when I did *Allegiance* and he said, "he's [Stafford] the first Canadian Asian to direct a Broadway musical". And I was so embarrassed. I remember saying to the publicist, "can you please have them retract this from the website?" He said, "why"? And I said, "I find this embarrassing. I'm just a kid from Toronto. Is this true that I'm the first?" And he said, "yes, it is true, obviously." And he said, "you have to understand that, as being that first Canadian Asian, you're showing that to not only the rest of the world, but specifically the rest of Canada and the other Staffords that exist in Canada." Most Asian families aren't pushing their kids to become artists or saying screw Canada and move to New York. It was really interesting because I started to realize, with your book, and with my picture connected to Theatre Calgary, that there is a ten-year-old, twelve-year-old, eighteen-year-old who's going to look at that picture and go, oh, I'm Japanese, Asian, Korean, Black, and if they can do it, then I guess I can do it. That is important now. It's more important than anything because it's the future. The future of our industry is going to make sure that the Seans and the Staffords don't go, "I don't see myself, so it must be impossible and I'll become an accountant."

**So did the move to New York arise out of your work with Livent and the connections that you had made in terms of the big companies?**

As I said, I graduated in 1992 from York University, and kind of immediately delved into my job as receptionist secretary with regards to Livent. It was really important for me to share with Garth that I was more interested in the artistic or production side of things because I was pretty much focused on the administrative side. So I had a conversation with him and said to him that I was really interested in seeing if I could get something over on the production side, and he discouraged me. He said, "if you want to work in press full time, that's a much better thing for you". I didn't really appreciate it, but I wasn't upset. I realized I hit the glass ceiling. I worked there, I proved myself as a good colleague, from receptionist to secretary to press assistant. But he saw something more for me, or he saw something that he felt was the right thing. And I didn't really believe in that. So what I did was pretty risky. I acknowledged it and I said that I didn't want to work for the company any longer in that capacity. He didn't bat an eyelash. Garth is the type of person who would say, you're making a mistake, but bye. The next thing I did was as a production assistant for the Canadian premiere of *Miss Saigon* in 1993. That was an amazing entry point into how something as big as *Miss Saigon* was built from page to stage. During that time, I had heard about this revival called *Show Boat* that was coming to Toronto produced by the company that I once worked for. Some would call it a lot of moxie and chutzpah, but I found myself writing a letter to Hal Prince basically saying, you're coming here, I'm here, I'll do anything. And, lo and behold, I got a call from Arlene Caruso at the Hal Prince organization, who said, "I have Hal Prince on the phone for Stafford Arima." And that journey began. I'd never assisted someone. I mean, Hal Prince. This was the director that directed *Evita*, the show that introduced me to theatre.

**Especially at this stage in the early 90s, too, he had been through the paces at this point. So that's a big deal.**

Yes, for sure. And in comes Garth on the first day of rehearsals, crossing right in front of me. Acknowledges Hal, looks behind, just looked at me and smiled and shook his head kind of like, of course. He didn't say it, but in so many ways, I think his brain was going, only you could make this happen. So Hal had his trusted Ruthie Mitchell, who was his right-hand person for many decades. And then from that extraordinary experience, being part of the creation of this immense show with over sixty people on the stage with Susan Stroman, hot off the heels of *Crazy For You*. Just to be in this room with Eugene Lee. I was a sponge soaking, soaking, soaking it in. The late, great Elaine Stritch was in the show and I remember, Hal said to me, "I want you to go work with Elaine. Refresh her on the blocking and the lines." Literally just said it and said, "do it." So I went to the PSM and said we need to book a room, and was in the rehearsal. I get there and Hal and Stro were in a different room doing one of the big numbers, and in walks Elaine with her white shirt and her Black tights and glasses. And the first thing she says to me is, "where the fuck is Hal?" And I said, "he's, you know, with Stro right now." And she said, What is this for?" And I said, "oh you know, we're just reviewing some stuff." And she went on a tirade. I mean, yelling, cursing. She was upset. I don't remember what she said, I just remember that she saw red. And I saw fear. And she was in my face. I just remember thinking, what am I doing? I don't know what to do. I don't know what to do. This is Elaine Stritch. And I then did something that I guess could have made or broke my entire career is, I said, "Elaine, just shut the fuck up." And she paused for three and three quarters seconds, that perfect pause. And she cracked a huge smile. And she said, "you're with me, kid."

**Holy shit.**

We weren't close friends, but we got closer. And I remember asking Hal a long time later, "why did you do that? Why did you throw me into the lion's den?" And he said, "Stafford, if you want to learn how to direct, you have got to learn how to work with the Elaine Stritchs." That kind of mentorship was very different. Sometimes, today, some of the incredible emerging artists see mentorship very differently. They need to sit down with you and you have to teach them everything and you have to tell them everything. No one told me how to work with Hal Prince. No one passed me a booklet and said this is what Hal wants and needs. And so that was quite an extraordinary experience. And then of course, because I'd worked with Stroman, she said her husband, who was Mike Ockrent at the time, is coming to direct *Crazy For You* at the Royal Alex. And he needs an assistant. Would you like to assist Mike on *Crazy For You*? I said, yes, thank you. So it went from *Saigon*, *Show Boat* to *Crazy For You*.

After *Crazy For You*, there was a reading of this new musical that was being developed by Livent based on a book by E. L. Doctorow. I wanted to be on that project because what I was really interested in was how to take a 270-page novel and turn that into a musical. So, I was on the very first reading of *Ragtime* in, 1995. I called myself the vice president of Xeroxing. I was in a room in downtown Toronto with a huge photocopier and I lived in that room. I should have had the face masks that we wear today because I was inhaling these Xerox fumes, and that's all I did. I didn't work with the director, I wasn't in the rehearsals; I was literally in that room 95 percent of the time copying script pages, music pages, collating. That was my job. From that, we did a second reading. Terrence McNally, said, "I need an assistant. Would you like to assist me?" Now, of course, I didn't want to be a writer. But I was like, oh, my gosh, I've graduated from the Xerox room and now I'm at a computer with Terrence. That's what I did. On the second reading, I assisted Terrence and Lynn (Ahrens). I remember Lynn and Terrence used to hand me these handwritten notes and rewrites. And, because of my experience as a secretary, I knew how to type pretty well. I used to do these pages for Lynn and Terrence and they used to laugh and they would be like, what? It took you a minute? And Lynn used to say, I'm always going to check for the errors. Terrence and I are going to find an error somewhere—but they didn't. LOL!

**What happened from there?**

Then I graduated from that on to assisting Frank Galati, who was the director, and then moved to an assistant resident director job in Toronto, and then moved to New York with the show as the assistant resident director for the Broadway production. The contract was open ended. I always thought, okay, if the show runs a year or two or three or whatever, I'll stay here, and then I'll come back to Toronto. But obviously, that didn't happen. So the journey of *Ragtime* from the Xerox boy, to being asked by Terrence, Lynn, and Stephen (Flaherty), to direct the West End production of *Ragtime*. And I remember when Terrence called me; I said, oh, is Frank not available? Meaning, you want me to remount the show in London? And he said, well, it's an interesting scenario. The producer wants a brand new version. We want a scaled down version, a minimalist version. And Lynn, Stephen, and I thought that we would like you to do it. I mean, can you imagine? It's a great reminder of relationships. You think, oh, I'm a Xerox boy? No, I'm not going to be in a Xerox room. I'm Stafford Arima. I just assisted Hal Prince. I just graduated from York. I shouldn't be in a Xerox room. I didn't know by being in a Xerox room that I would inevitably, some ten years later, direct a West End production. You don't think that way. But what I can look back at is on the importance of the working relationship of meeting a writer like Terrence and doing good work for him. I didn't make mistakes. I didn't speak out of turn. So, that was the journey to New York and that journey didn't end for twenty years.

That's amazing. And that's the nature of our business is you can end up in a room with a person one day who you think is completely irrelevant to your career or your path, and they could be the person that ends up literally changing the arc of your career in your life, which is pretty tremendous.

Well, it's kind of funny when you say it like that, because one could almost say, watch out for the Xerox boy. Watch out for the receptionist, because the receptionist became a director, but also an artistic director for a major theatre company in Canada. So, never underestimate those receptionists or those production assistants. Working with Marin Mazzie on *Ragtime*. I mean, Marin Mazzie was Marin Mazzie. I was a Xerox boy, slash maybe an assistant. And who would ever know that, ten years later, I would be directing her in *Carrie*. Those are relationships and journeys that are very, very important.

**How did the shows you worked on come about?**

Well, I went from *Ragtime*, which closed in just under two years, and then again, because of relationships and because Steven and Lynn's next project was *Seussical*, I became the Associate Director for *Seussical* in for the Boston tryout in 2000. And then, inevitably that ill-fated Broadway production also in 2000. So I stayed within the Flaherty, Ahrens, Galati family for *Seussical*. After that closed, I found work through more contacts. There was a musical based on the lyricist Ed Kleban called *A Class Act* that had a run at the Manhattan Theatre Club in 2000. Then it moved to Broadway in 2001 at the Ambassador Theatre. So then I went from associate directing *Seussical* to the Associate Director position on *A Class Act* with Lonny Price and that great group of people that was there.

I think I became known as a really good assistant, because the truth is all these are just fancy titles. Associate director, resident director, personal assistant. They're all basically assistant jobs because I'm not directing the work. I'm either assisting a director or maintaining a production. So, for quite a long time, I didn't direct. I just became known as this really good assistant. And if you looked at my résumé back then, it would have gone back to Hal Prince, to Mike Ockrent, Frank Galati, Lonny Price, and actually even Rob Marshall because when he took over for *Seussical* in New York. That was a pretty exciting group of people. So, when someone looked at that résumé, I didn't have a lot on my résumé but I guess I had some heavy hitters. I just feel so blessed to have had the opportunity to work with, these geniuses! It was a very different mentality than it is today. But assisting was what I was known for. I remember when Disney approached me about a resident directing one of their international shows. And then Terrence called me and he said, I want you to meet Jack O'Brien. He's doing a new musical based on *The Full Monty*. And Terrence wrote the book and so he said, I want you to meet Jack. I then realized that I had to make a move, because if I want to direct, I have to do something. So I turned down the meeting with Jack. I said no to Disney. I'd walk around the streets and people would always be saying, how's Hal? And then I moved away from Hal and toward Frank. They'd say, how's Frank doing? I started to realize that people look at me and go, Hal or Frank. Nothing wrong with that. However, I wanted to be looked at and go, oh, what are you directing?

**It's an interesting thing because there's the idea that as you march through this career, and as you climb the ladder, you start to contend with where you say yes or no to certain things. People will still call you for assistant work even though you think you're an associate. So do you just say no when the phone rings asking you to be an assistant and say, I only do associate work at this point? It's a hard choice.**

It's very hard. It's hard because sometimes people don't want to say no. I mean, it's employment. I've had these conversations with swings. They become known as the ultimate swing, so when the casting directors have to find a swing, we say, call Bobo and LoLo, because those are the best swings. But these swings want to get out of that job. However, then the swings make a lot of money because they're covering 85,000 parts. I remember Deidre Goodwin, an amazing Broadway dancer. I was always so impressed with Deidre because at one point she said, no more. I'm not just going to be in the ensemble. And I remember she auditioned for me and I was so impressed by the fact that she said, "enough".

I think, inevitably, the big change for me was when I was asked to direct the West End premiere of *Ragtime* in 2003. I was still doing assisting work up until that point and then came back to *Ragtime* with this amazing, amazing gift. Lynn and Stephen and Terrence, I owe them my career. I really, really do. From the days of Toronto when I worked for Garth, I owed that company a lot too. So in 2003, I did *Ragtime*. I was nominated for an Olivier Award. I remember that Sonia Friedman called me when I was at home in New York. And she said, "this is going to sound like an insult, but we're just really surprised." And I said, "what do you mean?" And she said, "it's just quite unorthodox for, basically, a foreigner in their first West End Show to be nominated for an Olivier Award." I remember when I was there, I didn't want to win. I was so scared of getting up in front of these people and I probably had that imposter feeling that I just don't deserve this. Who am I? I'm a kid from Toronto, please. But that credit allowed me to get my green card. So from 2000 to 2003, it was three years of, how do I get visas? How do I stay here? I didn't have relatives who live there [in the US], so it was three years of scrappy figuring it out. 2003 was the beginning of when people started to just slightly look at me a little differently. From then, it really was probably in 2005, when *Altar Boyz* opened and I became the *Altar Boyz* director.

**You live in Calgary now. Do you miss New York at all?**

Yeah, for lots of reasons, I miss it. But I think after spending twenty years there, I always say to people, New York has the best of everything and the worst of everything. It is completely polarized. I had a really amazing journey of twenty years there with no regrets. This next journey of being an artistic director was a kind of fitting time. Five years ago, forty-five came into office. And I just thought, I don't know. I remember everyone would say to me, you can leave. And I thought, maybe it's not a bad time to just take a break. Not a bad time, just to take a pause. I miss a lot of people. I miss the history of that city. But I don't miss it right now. And partly, that's because I have a job that I have to do and help shepherd this company [Theatre Calgary] through this pandemic.

**So, now you're Artistic Director of one of the biggest and most well-known regional theatres in Canada. What was that process like for you in terms of saying yes? And now that you're there, how do you reflect on what you've done before and what you want to do now moving forward in your career?**

I never wanted to be an artistic director. I didn't think I could be one. I think the artistic directors that I had the privilege of working for, Oskar Eustis at the Public, Barry Edelstein at The Globe: these to me are artistic directors. You walk into their office, and there's every Shakespeare folio there and they could quote all of the soliloquies. I'm just like, ". . . Sweeney Todd?" So I just never thought I would. It was never in my periphery. But when the call came, I said, why not? Why not go out for it? So I went out for it. The search committee asked me to curate a couple of seasons, so I did. And I thought about it obviously, but I was just going to be me. And

I didn't walk in with a tie. I saw a picture of the previous artistic director and he had a tie, a suit. I said, I'm going to come in my Obi-Wan robe, my hair was down and I just did me. I didn't really know what it meant to be an artistic director. I knew on the surface. But, now, I really look at the role as it's not just about what's the season and what's this and that. It's about helping navigate a company. There's a healing process that occurs when we do art. We reveal to heal. And, through those awakenings, I think it's possible to help shape a community, help change a community, help bring some diversity to a community. So I think that is what I'm excited and interested about, rather than just picking the shows. That's important.

But, again, the programming is going to help that trajectory. In my first season, the majority of the subscribers were very upset with me. My first show that I programmed in my first season was an original play written by a Calgary writer, Tara Beagan, who is an Indigenous writer. That was, I guess, too much for the current climate. Then I did a world premiere of a new musical called *Mary and Max* that was based on the film. And then we did a world premiere of *Boom X* by Toronto writer, Rick Miller. So three world premieres in one season. To me, that was exciting, but there was a desire for more recognizable titles. So the ship isn't going to turn in one season. It's really going to take probably a few years. Now, what the Covid experience did, is that it's been like a bit of a reset. So, I think in many ways, we have an opportunity, through our messaging and in our onboarding of the subscribers, find ways to push, nudge, massage. Last year, I programmed a Canadian musical called *The Louder We Get* written by two Calgarians: Colleen and Akiva. It was an LGBTQ2S+ story. Marc Hall, an Ontario kid, wanted to take his boyfriend to the prom. It had been thirty-one years since an LGBTQ2S+ story had been on Theatre Calgary's stage. Thirty-one years.

**That's generational loss at that point.**

That's right. So I wanted to change it up. I remember saying to the board, we might get bomb threats. I don't know. We didn't, thankfully. So, those are small victories, but important ones and ones that I'm excited about.

**It speaks to the need to have artistic leadership right at the top that understands that. I think that's one of the biggest things as an industry right now: that we're grappling with this notion of change can happen from the ground up, of course, but it also does need to**

happen from the top down. Everybody's hands have got to be on it. Even just to be so considerate to look at something in full view and say, let's make sure that we've got the stories we need. Because that's our obligation in the theatre. That's what we have to do.

And the name of our city is in our title. We're called Theatre Calgary. It's so important for us to represent all of Calgary. And Calgary is not just one faction or type of demographic. It's a rainbow color of lots of people, ages, colors, sizes, creeds. It's really important for me and my new partner, Maya Choldin, to explore those stories and to make those changes. Slowly, but with intention.

**What is your hope for, not only Theatre Calgary, but your legacy? You've already amassed a legacy of different types of work in this industry. I'm curious, with this pandemic and the pause we've been in and given the conversations around everything that's been going on—what does the future hold?**

I think it's made me more vocal than I think I've ever been prior to Black Lives Matter. When I worked in New York City, I remember there were a couple of times you'd go there and someone would be like, "hey, pass the egg rolls", or some stupid thing. But I never felt as an artist that I was only hired to do Asian shows. Or not hired to do non-Asian shows. I was known as the Canadian. That's what most people thought of me as. Not as Asian, gay, overweight. A lot of my colleagues have been marginalized because of their skin color. So I think it's important that people understand and see that a gay person of color can not only direct a show on Broadway, but can also be an artistic leader for a major theatre company in Canada. If that gives hope to the future of our industry, to directors, artistic directors, designers and writers and casting directors, producers, musicians, arrangers, then that might be my little contribution.

I think that the work that Maya and I are going to do at Theatre Calgary is going to work on the rusted bolts that are in the theatre. We're getting at them, we're wiggling them and we're cleaning off all the rust, and, maybe by the time we leave with the foundation, the bedrock will be a little off kilter, so that the next team can come in and even lift it. I think it's foolish to think that, in five years, everything's going to change and be better. But the hard work of cleaning out all that rust and that bedrock is exciting. I want to pave the way for the next team and give them something so that they don't have to bring out the Spic and Span.

**That's the true work of it. Of course, there's an eagerness right now to want to respond so immediately, but we need to be aware of the trauma and that work that has been done to set these things in place. That will also take time to undo if we want it to undo it in a way that's actually meaningful and goes to the root. Going back to New York for a moment: how did *Allegiance* come about and what was that whole process like?**

Well, I was involved in 2010 on the first real reading when they first brought on a director. My father's side of the family was interned during the Second World War in Vancouver. So this story was very personal to me. From 2010, we workshopped it and developed it, and then we had our premiere at the Old Globe in 2012. It took three years to get to New York after that. What brings me a tremendous amount of pride is it probably will be the first and only internment musical that will ever hit Broadway. I think what that show reminds me of is that, when anyone says "no" or when someone says, "why are you doing that?" your answer is, "well, why not?" "There should never be a show on Broadway about the internment." "That's going to be a real humdinger of a musical." "You shouldn't do it."

The producer Lorenzo Thione and all of us surrounded ourselves with people who said nothing is impossible. If we want to grab a tagline from Yentl: nothing's impossible, and from a Mariah Carey song: make it happen. That's inevitably what we did. And, for the story, it wasn't George Takei's life, but George had been in an internment camp as a young boy. It was really important that we brought to light an historical event that happened in the United States to reveal; to heal. There's also a deep history in Canada, but it's got a specific history as an American story. It's funny, because I think if the show opened recently, when everything was happening, I think it would have been responded to very differently than how it was responded to in 2015, which was when we were just on the cusp of talking about immigration. Then, of course, everything blew up later with Donald Trump. But there were so many victories about that show: we had our composer who was Asian, the director was Asian, the sound designer was Asian, the associate director was Asian, the SDC intern was Asian. So five people on the creative team were Asian, and then a 98 percent all Asian cast, where we had over maybe nine Broadway debuts. Those statistics are something that I didn't really think about back then. Back in 2015, 2014, 2012, I wasn't thinking, I've got to get this, I've got to get that. I just wanted the best, most appropriate people. And that's who we got. Now I look back at it and go, wow. How many Broadway shows have the director, the composer, the sound designer, and the associate director all Asian?

So that brings me a tremendous amount of pride to be part of history in that way—not just because it was the first internment musical (and maybe the last), and not even because it was my debut as a Broadway director. I look at it with a different lens now. That lens really is how important it is to manifest creative stories that can be elevated to Broadway or the West End, and to be able to tell a story that gives insight into one: something that happened, and two: a story about a family that happens to be Japanese American, and make that a universal story. When I direct in Tokyo or in Korea, you know what their favourite musical is? *Fiddler on the Roof*. Do they have many Jewish people in Korea? No. But they know what tradition is. They know what family is. So directing *Allegiance*, it had its flaws; it's not that it's the perfect musical but, that stuff aside, it really comes down to the point that that show made it to Broadway. And it made it even though everyone said it couldn't go, or it shouldn't go because no one's going to buy a ticket to see an internment musical. So, it's a great reminder for anyone that, if you believe in something, you can [Mariah] make it happen.

**This book will hopefully be a book that sits on the shelves of a lot of arts libraries and schools and places where young artists can get it. If you had advice to offer, or something that you wish you had heard at the early stages of the game, particularly as an artist of color, what would you want to make sure that somebody doesn't miss in reading this?**

Never give up. Never give up. That tenacious spirit that lives within us all, especially in this industry, can be squelched, can be suffocated immediately. But if you really want to do this and love it, and there's nothing else that you can imagine but the industry, whether it's just theatre or film or music, just never give up. The other part of that is: let go and let God. I don't mean that in a religious way, but in a way that if you come to a crossroads at any point in your career, age twenty-four, forty-eight, sixty-two, and you decide, I'm going to pivot; I've enjoyed my forty years as a Broadway dancer, I am now going to open a flower shop: Great! *Carrie* being revived in 2012 was a result of never giving up. I was told by everyone once again, no, you can't do it; who are you? A-List directors want to direct *Carrie*. I'm not an A-List director. I know that, I'm not a fool. But I just wanted to do it because I believed in that message. I believed in the power of the relevance of that story today being different. That's probably a little thread in the work that I've done. Even *Altar Boyz*; they're like fish out of water. Right? These are Catholic boys singing in a boy band. *Carrie* was a good example of me wanting to do it and so I made it happen. Granted, with a lot of good fortune and serendipity, but just because someone said to me "you can't do it because you're not an A-List director" doesn't mean that I took that and said okay. Just like Garth said to me: "no, no, you can't work in production. Stay in administration." Never give up. I don't know if anyone ever said that to me. What about you? What would be your answer?

**That's funny, no one's ever asked it back. I think the latter part of your answer, let go and let God, is great. Knowing that, somewhere along the way, you have to believe that where you're meant to be is where you're meant to be. Especially in this industry. Otherwise you'll go absolutely nuts. I music direct for Andre De Shields and his iconic phrase is "The top of one mountain is the bottom of the next, so keep climbing." To hear that from him after fifty plus years of doing this type of work is super informative. This work of constant, constant rediscovery of who you are. You can spend fifteen years doing that, and then realize, oh, wow, look at how different of a person I am. I think you channel through what the universe needs you to do in your time here. But that's an impossible thing to think about when you're nineteen or twenty; when you're at that stage in the game, and all the world is telling you to do is to prove yourself and be okay with that.**

**I remember being in my early twenties and I was doing an internship, and an MD said, "it took me a long time to realize that I wouldn't be a young MD until I was thirty." I laugh at that now being over that marker, but certainly, time and experience and age is just something that you just can't replace. Learning to be thankful for the journey and getting there. Be proud of a résumé that shows the length of the road to get there and not just trying to have it show the top of the mountain. Having it shows the fact that you had to climb the mountain to get there. And that's tough realizing that everyone's done that. Even the people we all idolize.**

You're very wise for your stage of life. I don't know if I was wise like you. I think I just did it on some sort of instinct. I didn't have mentors. I didn't have the books. I didn't have the people that I could really speak to. I was always very in awe of the people that I worked with at a very early age because I was working with the Hal Princes. And, again, I would always say to someone: never underestimate the impact of a relationship. It's not about being nice to people so you can get jobs; it's just about not underestimating relationships because you never know.

**In the same vein, everybody comes to the table to make the thing equally as good from all angles. It doesn't matter. I don't care if you're the fourth props master. This wouldn't happen without you. It is truly a team effort. I think that's a cool thing on an artistic level. It's cool to be in a line of work where you have to have the ability to work collectively for the greater good.**

Well, with your book, I hope it becomes the Bible for this next generation. The fact that you're opening up, you're parting the curtain, and allowing people to see inside behind the scenes, but with an array of faces that don't look like the books of thirty years ago is huge. So that young person who's going to open Sean Mayes' book is maybe a young Black kid from Scarborough, Ontario, who thinks, maybe I can do it. Maybe I have a shot. I hope and believe that what Obama being in that White House signaled, and Ms. Harris being VP, it's got to do something. It might not change everything today but it's definitely different than thirty years ago. I think the advice I would give is to buy Sean Mayes' book.

**Well, thank you, Stafford. And thank you for your time!**

# ALEX LACAMOIRE

 **Alex Lacamoire** is a Tony, Grammy, Emmy, and Olivier Award-winning orchestrator, music director, arranger, and composer. He is best known for his work on Broadway's critically-acclaimed shows *Hamilton*, *Dear Evan Hansen*, and *In The Heights*, and FX's mini-series "Fosse/ Verdon." Lacamoire currently serves as the Music Supervisor and Conductor for the Broadway revival of Stephen Sondheim's *Sweeney Todd* (starring Josh Groban and Annaleigh Ashford), which features Jonathan Tunick's original orchestrations played by a twenty-six-piece orchestra. Lacamoire's other credits as music director, arranger, and/or orchestrator include: *The Wrong Man* (Off-Broadway), *Bring It On*, *9 to 5* (Drama Desk and Grammy noms), *Wicked*, *Bat Boy*, and *Godspell* (2001 national tour). He also served as the Executive Music Producer for many films including *The Greatest Showman*, *In The Heights*, *VIVO*, *Dear Evan Hansen*, and *Tick, Tick . . . Boom!* Lacamoire is the winner of three Tony Awards for Best Orchestrations, four Grammy Awards (three for Best Musical Theatre Album and one for Best Compilation Soundtrack For Visual Media), three Olivier Awards for Outstanding Achievement in Music, and an Emmy Award for Outstanding Music Direction on "Fosse/Verdon." In 2019, he received an Honorary Doctorate of Music from his alma mater, Berklee College Of Music. He was also the recipient of a

first-of-its-kind Kennedy Center Honors for his contribution to Hamilton. Lacamoire and the *Hamilton* creative team were honored as the "trailblazing creators of a transformative work that defies category"—a distinction never before awarded by the arts institution. In 2023, he was named an Official Yamaha Artist. Lacamoire currently resides in New York.

**When did you realize that it was musical theatre that you could use your talents and skills for?**

I had a very specific moment where I thought of theatre as a thing for me in junior high school. I was playing in the pit for the school summer production of *Bye Bye Birdie*, and I was playing bass. Keyboard bass, mind you.

**Wow.**

And here I was playing in a band, which is fun to begin with. I got to play with a drummer, a sax player, and a piano in an ensemble setting. But on top of that, I was looking up at the stage and seeing my peers performing, singing and dancing, and being part of this collective whole. And I just loved it, because I knew these from my classes where I saw them as "normal" kids like me. There they were on stage doing something I couldn't do. And I was supplying something that *they* couldn't do. So I just love that we were completely genuine, and through that I also just loved how outgoing theatre kids were. I always say that practicing music is a solitary ambition. You're in a practice room by yourself, and you're going over scales and you're repeating. You're doing a lot of stuff by rote, but there's something about practicing with someone else that I just found so much fun.

**That's really cool!**

Yeah, and as the years went on, I found that I really enjoyed theatre music. Particularly the rock stuff. Once I found out about *Pippin*, and *Godspell*, that really appealed to me. This is around the time that *Les Mis* and *Phantom* were becoming a thing. So just enough pop in it that it got me interested. I think it helped that I kept getting asked to accompany people for things. It just became clear that there were other pianists around me and *they* weren't getting asked. There's something about the way that I played that my peers seemed to like, I suppose. Even in high school; we did our high school production of *West Side Story* and I had never played it before. And they asked me to be a pianist for rehearsals. So I had gotten used to being asked to gig, really. To be a part of the process. I just love that. And I just also liked that, "Hey, I am the pianist, the one providing the music for all these other people needing to learn how to sing or these other people needing to dance or these run throughs," or whatever it was. I felt important. And I loved that.

**Where did the shift happen after high school?**

I studied jazz and classical and went to Berklee before Berklee had a theatre program, so it didn't seem like theatre was going to be a career for me. But, again, I kept getting put in situations where I was asked to do things, and I came up on a job working for Boston Conservatory, playing voice lessons. I got asked to be in the band for the Boston Conservatory production of *Pippin*, even though I was still at Berklee. So I was always kind of moonlighting as a theatre person, playing auditions in town for regional theatre, for Huntington Theatre Company in Boston, for the Harvard production of *A Little Night Music*. These are institutions that had nothing to do with Berklee and yet I was gigging at them.

**Seems like you were a natural.**

It's hard to say if this is my calling. I feel like I'm good at it. I feel like it's something that I love. But I think, more importantly, something connected with me. The way that I played the music, the way that I play the repertoire, seemed to connect with the people who were asking me to play. So there was some kind of transaction happening. Everybody was getting a need met, if you will. And that's how I found my way to it.

**You seem to be a master collaborator, and that as a role, even within the realm of music in theatre, has really been the reason why you've been this creator of all of these amazing pieces that are the big works of our art.**

Thank you for saying that. I think it comes out of respect that all these different departments are coming together to create something. And I know we talked about the collaborative process. If you were at a symphony orchestra, obviously, there is a machine at play. There's the string section, there's the wind section, there's the brass section. Everybody's working at once to make something unified out of disparate elements. Totally cool. But theatre takes it a step further because you have lights going along with costumes, going along with a stage manager, going along with a conductor. All of these even more disparate mediums are all coming together to create a whole. So once you realize you're working with this lighting person and you're paying attention to what it is that they do, you respect them in a different way. You see a costume designer make something out of nothing, you respect them in a certain way. For example, I always wanted to dance and it wasn't until I started trying to learn how to dance myself, that I realized how not cut out for it I am. Then you realize, "They're doing something that I can't do." And once you see enough shows, and compare lights from one set to another, you start to realize what that looks like. You start to pay attention to deeper parts of process, to what's happening and what kind of decisions are being made. And you start to think to yourself, "This isn't what I'd make if I were at this juncture." You start to realize how all of these choices impact what the whole is.

**Ultimate collaboration.**

Yeah. I also think it comes from having worked on shows or seen enough workshops that when you're standing at a music stand and delivering text, singing a song and making people forget the real world around them, it's one thing. But: if all the elements aren't on the same page or telling the same story, it could throw everything askew. If you don't have the right costume design, if your choreographer doesn't have the same vision that the director does, something's not going to be in alignment. So I feel fortunate that I've worked on projects where there is alignment and there is a unified goal. And that comes from having a really strong and wonderful director that is able to round everything up and get the team moving in the same direction. It comes from working with designers that are at the top of their field, who also resonate with the project and respect the project and respect each other. I thrive when the team is well put-together and when excellent human beings fit together. And that's where you realize what your part is in all of it. And it's just this mutual respect. And, when mutual admiration happens in a show, that's where I really enjoy the collaborative process. This is to say nothing about the collaboration with the actors; I'm talking strictly about the design level. That's a whole other topic and paragraph.

**By virtue of the projects that you've done, you've crafted a lot of new work specifically. Is there any part of that process that you admire the most in terms of what you do or have done with it?**

I do love all of it, honestly, Sean. It's hard to pinpoint one specific moment because they all have their charms for me. The early, early stages are glorious because you're still finding the piece, you get to see the composer create, recreate, throw away, adapt. And if the composers are open enough, that's where my favorite part starts to come in. That's where the way I play music can influence what the counterpoint might be, what the band might be, what the [instrumental] hits might be, what the arrangement could be. So I do love that. It is also very fun to be in the room to teach vocals. I love sitting behind a piano and teaching people harmonies and hearing what something sounds like after everyone has worked apart. I love that.

**Such a rewarding moment of the process.**

Yes, and I love the performance part of it as well. If I'm actually at the podium conducting and leading the band, being in the "run" part of it is great. The orchestration process can be tedious. But I find that part to be really fun when I've lived with a project long enough that the decisions are relatively easy to make. I lived with the opening number of *In the Heights* for so long. We had enough workshops to know where everything was going that, when it came time to actually notate parts on a staff, the ideas were going to flow. So, I do love when we get to do that. I love the sitzprobe, I love the band rehearsal, I love the opening night, all that stuff, it's all great fun. That's why I think I enjoy having such a holistic view of big shows that I work on. I do enjoy that I get to have input in all the decisions about the arrangements, the orchestration, the conducting and all of that because I have some feelings and opinions about them. And I think to myself, "Oh, I know how I'd like this to go." It is liberating to be the one that it all funnels through. Not to say that I wouldn't collaborate in other ways, but I find it's easier for me to kind of oversee it all and do it all at the same time. It's more difficult physically because I need to sleep and you're working crazy hours and not resting. But at the end of the day, when you get to sit back and be like, "oh, wow, I had input in all of this", it's a very gratifying feeling.

**I think one of the cool things in what you've done is that you have sat behind the podium as a conductor, and as an MD behind a lot of your own arrangements, both instrumentally and vocally. What was the journey of coming to this work and finding the skillset to be able to do that?**

I would say it's a couple of things. The first thing is, I got the opportunities because I raised my hand. Period. Full stop. And I was able to raise my hand because I had built up the confidence due to my curiosity, growing up and being obsessed with music. So that manifested itself in many ways. For example: I remember being obsessed with *Pippin* and owning the vocal score. As you play the piano, you see the cue notes for all these other instruments, all these scales that the strings are playing, all these lines that the flutes are playing. So I just *needed* to know what that all sounded like together. I remember before I had a four track machine, before I had a sequencer, I would record myself playing the piano part, and then overdub myself playing the flute lines on piano while the cassette was in *another* boombox. And I'd go back and forth multiple times to build up—and it sounded like crap.

**[*Laughs.*] Wow, that's going back, especially with the cassettes!**

That was my pastime, Sean. That's how I had fun. Instead of going outside and playing football, this is what I would do! [*Laughter.*] I have memories of staying up till five in the morning, transcribing the piano part of a Cutting Crew song. I remember sitting with the guitar until the wee hours of the morning to try to figure out the tuning for a Led Zeppelin song that I loved just because I wanted to know how to play it. When I got a keyboard, it had a digital sequencer; the Korg 01/WFD. I would build sequences of my favorite Rush songs. My favorite Zeppelin songs. I have learned to play drums on the keyboard. Sometimes people would ask me to build sequences *for* them. I still remember a friend in high school who wanted a karaoke version of a Harry Connick Jr. song. So I transcribed the big band arrangement and played it on my keyboard. I played the trumpet patch, played the sax patch, played the drums and I learned it all. And that's because I was just curious. Vocal harmonies, Yes songs and Queen songs, transcribing them because I wanted to know how they did it so that I could maybe, one day, get a bunch of friends together and create it. So, I did all that and it led to me just having a competence around vocal arranging and arranging such that, when it came time to create my own charts, I was ready. That's why once I got to New York, and an opportunity like *Bat Boy* came along, my question was, so who's going to orchestrate it? Well, by then I had enough of a relationship with Larry O'Keefe that he was able to say, "Alex should orchestrate it. He can do this." And we created it together. And that, again, gave me the confidence to keep doing a number of other projects.

**Do you have any sort of process as far as journaling or jotting ideas down in a very specific way to keep your creativity on a page or in a place where you can return to it?**

I just go. I've never really journaled. I am starting to regret that I haven't journaled. I always thought "oh, my memory is fantastic. I'll remember all this stuff." But I do keep everything. I have drafts and drafts of old piano vocals so, if ever I'm curious, I trace back to what was given to me or what the first draft of something was and get to see what came out of it. So it's nice to revisit that way. And the work was fun to edit.

**With your work outside of theatre now, on the movie screen being just one example, how does that influence your drive and your skill as an artist in general?**

Well, I will say this: I have not done a new piece of theatre since all the TV and film work that I've done. So I don't know how it's affected how I do theatre, but I do know theatre has completely affected how I do TV and film. Objective storytelling, music arranging, and how music can tell the story. So that is very much a part of how I create stuff. It was amazing just learning the translation between TV/film and theatre. There are definitely some similarities, but things don't overlap as much as you would think they would. So, I'm still navigating what that is and still learning how differently everyone does something. I think my big lesson has been thinking that there's one way to do a movie, one way to do a TV show. And I have been fortunate enough to have done enough projects now to know that every studio is different, every person is different, every process is different. So, you've just got to be nimble and loose, and learn how to anticipate what's coming. I think a big lesson for me is, that in theatre, there's a lot of familiarity and a lot of assumptions made that, other people will take care of certain things, because that's their department. And they've done that enough times. I keep learning more and more that, in TV and film, you have to ask for what it is that you want. And you have to anticipate the things that perhaps only a stage manager thought of before. Things that perhaps only the contractor thought of before.

**One of the coolest things about your career is that it's kind of impossible to think up any of these shows and not have you be right there. Do you consider the fact that that is really your legacy to the American musical theatre and that you've changed the arc of this forever? Do you think about that in terms of the future and what your hope is for the art moving forward?**

Well, first off, thanks for the kind words. I will say this: I always think to myself, "I'm just really lucky." And I feel like I met Lin-Manuel just at the right time. I met Pasek and Paul when they were about to break out with [*Dear Evan*] *Hansen*. And, you know, I was already a fan of Stephen

Schwartz when he asked me to be involved with *Wicked*, and all those things happened. I was born at that right time, I suppose. So I know that what I do is inextricably linked to what it is that they create. So, yes, I'm proud of what I've done. I feel like I hear my voice in the things that I've been a part of. And in terms of legacy, like you said, I'm extremely proud of that. I know what it is that I contributed to these things. And that's a hard thing to explain to folks and a hard thing for a non-musician to understand what that truly means.

**Absolutely. We work in the shadows often.**

That being said, that is fine. Because, again, I feel like I have done good work, because I am passionate about the projects I'm working on. I have chosen a practice that speaks to me, musically speaking. I can tell you, I still remember the first time I popped in the tape for *Bat Boy* and was like, "Oh, man, this music is awesome. I totally want to do this." Same thing for the early, early demos of *In the Heights*. I heard something in there. And I saw myself in it. I heard myself in it and I felt that I could contribute. And that was important to me. And, you know, the career of the MD is a very tricky thing because everybody's skill sets are different and everybody's level of involvement is different. Because the MD for a revival of the show, as you mentioned, is going to have a very different task than the MD for a new work. And whether that MD arranges or orchestrates or not will contribute to their level of involvement, and how specific a composer is will also contribute to the involvement of that MD. So it's a really hard thing to quantify, which is why I feel like it's hard to ever have an award for best music director.

**The debate around the music director's Tony being reopened perhaps . . .?!**

I know there's people out there who think there should be a Tony award for best music director, but I actually contend that it's a very hard thing to quantify. And I understand why there's not a category for it. And it's also very hard to point to what an MD does. You can point to what a choreographer does, you can see that. You can point to what a costume designer or what lighting has done, what a director has done, and they really do, I think, in a sense, create something out of nothing. And I do believe that orchestration and arranging is a derivative art form that we do because it is based on what the composer has created. So that is the reason why, I think, when The Public Theatre presents a programme, they don't mention the MD on the title page. That's why when you look outside at the marquee for *Hamilton*, you see Lin's name, Tommy's name, Blank's [Andy Blankenbuehler's] name, but not mine. And that's because what they did, they carry so much more on their shoulders than I ever will, and I acknowledge that. Because what Tommy [Kail] has to do as a director, and all the teams, with all the things that he has to manage and supervise and deal with . . . It's similar to what I do except a fraction of a fraction of a fraction of what he has on his mind. Same thing for Blankenbuehler. What he sees and what he does, I couldn't make. Whatever a choreographer creates can make or break a show. I had the fortune of having these really amazing demos from Lin, and real great suggestions about what kind of sound needed to exist on *Hamilton* and what he liked. So I helped shepherd and execute something. I know what my role is and I'm clear on what that is. And so, because of that, that's why I just always have gratitude that I got asked to join. I work with people who I admire, people who I respect, people who are veterans.

**What is your hope for students entering the field? What sort of advice would you give and is that advice different from before the pandemic to now afterwards?**

My advice pre-pandemic was always pretty much the same, which is this art form is meant for the people who really truly love it. And the amount of dedication and perseverance that one must have to succeed in this biz, in any of its departments, means you have to love it, and you have to really connect to it. So if you love it and connect with it then, by all means, go for it. If there's a skill that you can acquire, that you can get better at, practice that. If you play piano and you're not good at all the styles, then practice the styles that you're not good at. If you're an instrumentalist and your pocket isn't deep, then turn on that metronome and practice until it is. So, I think you just have to keep going. Have curiosity about the different styles and genres and how things are put together and have respect for it and pull it apart and learn from it. I think that's what I would do and I don't know if that advice is different post pandemic or not.

**Some of those skills are always essential to this work.**

For sure. I have been really moved by how, even during the shutdown, people were still finding ways to have readings on Zoom. People were still finding ways to record orchestrations separately from rooms and people were longing to connect and create music together, even if we weren't in the same room. And that, to me, is collaboration. And that is music and that is theatre and that is all of those things. So it's humbling to know that there's still a desire for theatre, that shows are still running, and despite the hit that the industry's taken, people still want to go see shows. And, even with tours, the shows are still out there. So it's still a respected art form. It is still an event, it is still an activity, it is still community and there's a performance to behold and people still respect that. That's been in place since ancient Greece. So that desire's still there. It's not going anywhere. So, like I said, you just got to go for it. That's my advice.

**It's interesting to think of those people of color who are coming up the ranks and thinking about this stuff. That's a pretty epic legacy to think of how some of the biggest pieces you've worked on have literally put more people of color at the forefront of theatre. Certainly, that wasn't the case when we were checking out what musical theatre movies look like. It was like, oh, I don't look like anyone in here. But now that's not the case. And that's expanding further and further on film, on stage. That must be a really special thing for you as well.**

I do love it and I feel grateful. And again, I trace it back to Lin-Manuel and the doors that he opened being who he is and showing up as who he is. Just so boldly being who he is. I mean, his writing, that's special. He's a genius. And because of that, because of his ability, because of how prolific he is, I think of all that has happened because of Lin. I think about *In the Heights*, I think about *Hamilton*, *Vivo*. The *In the Heights* movie as well as *Encanto*. The list goes on about all these things that he has had a hand in. It just lifted up works of color, and that's amazing. What moves me to tears sometimes, is seeing people who are now in their twenties who were teens or really young when *In the Heights* happened. And I'd like to think that that allowed them to feel represented in art in a way that they hadn't before. I don't know that I could say I've longed for that representation because you don't know what you don't know. But I do know that, had *In the Heights* been around when I was in high school, I would have lost my mind. And I know that. I remember that. I carry that with me.

**Do you have any hopes for the industry and for yourself as an artist in the next five to ten years in terms of what the road ahead looks like?**

My hope for the industry is that it continues on the trend. I feel like people are now hungry and more curious than they have been for diverse representation in work. Long may that continue. I know that there's a fear that what we're experiencing now is a fad or a pendulum swing or something. If it is, it doesn't matter to me because whatever comes out of this will plant seeds for more to come, for more to be normalized. So my assumption is that there's going to be a wave of interest in works of color in all mediums. I know that operas are now like, "where are all the Black composers?" And theatres are like, "Okay, where all the Latin composers", "what could we do?", "who are the Latin music directors?" So there's a search happening, and there's a hunger that I've not seen before. And that's tricky, right? Because we want to lift our folks and at the same time, we want the people who really deserve the gig. And you want those choices to be merit based.

**And the danger of that elevation before a point when people are ready as well, which can be more detrimental.**

Exactly. You want people to be set up to succeed. But I do think also, at the same time, there needs to be, I think, a big strong influx and injection of people into the sphere that had heretofore been without. And my hope is that more people will therefore see themselves represented and therefore be more interested or be more invested, and want to get into the circle that we love. Because, no matter what, the world of theatre is small. And Broadway is a small block radius that has a global impact. But the amount of musicians in the world, the amount of actors in the world, down to people who can dance, people who can sing, people who can act, the people who can dance *and* sing *and* act and be Latino. "Okay, you could be in *In the Heights*." And it gets even smaller, and smaller, and smaller. So it's concentric in that way. So all this to say, my hope is that it gets easier as time goes, but we'll see where that leads. So that's my hope.

**Is there anything for yourself, where you're thinking about how you're going to be involved with things for the next little while?**

Yeah, it's so funny. Like I told you, you've caught me at an interesting moment in time where I don't have anything firm planned out yet. And I'm totally fine with that. At the same time, there's still that insecurity that also lies in "the new", which is like, "Oh, God, when is my next gig going to be? Is Lin to call me for his next thing?" I am a freelancer, I acknowledge that. We all are. And you hope that the friendships that you have and the relationships we have persevere, because you know what it's like to work at a certain level and to fire at a certain cylinder, as you said.

**A difficult reality of looking for the next job that hits us all at any stage.**

Absolutely. So you long for that, and you hunger for that. And, yeah, there's always that hope that I will get to be involved with work that is that meaningful to me. And that's really what it's about, right? The impact that it has on the world: you can't control that. And you *hope* that it has the impact of the shows that I've worked on with Lin. But that might not always be the case. And I get that. So all I really care about is that I continue to work with artists who inspire me, with people who are good human beings, and collaborators that I respect.

**That's probably the best way to wrap up a chapter like this too, isn't it! If you really want it, you'll be ready to embrace all of the security and the insecurity that it will always bring, and that will always shape and craft what you do and create. If you go out in good faith and in good spirits, that will always keep you very busy, clearly!**

I appreciate it. You asked great questions. It was fun to talk to you about this. I feel like you talked about some stuff that I don't usually get into. So thanks for opening that door.

**Thank *you*!**

# JASON MICHAEL WEBB

2019 Special Tony Award recipient and Drama Desk winner, **Jason Michael Webb** is a composer, lyricist, musical director, producer, and arranger. From conducting orchestras in Broadway pits to writing and arranging music for a President's inauguration, Jason has dedicated his life to using music to heal, uplift, and encourage.

Mr. Webb's early musical training consisted of formal classical study, playing in small churches and listening to pop music. By twenty-one, he had a degree in classical piano, played in the biggest churches in New York City, and made his orchestral solo debut with the Queens Symphony.

He then went on to become Musical Director of the six-time Grammy Award-winning Brooklyn Tabernacle, for whom Mr. Webb co-wrote and produced four albums for The Brooklyn Tabernacle Choir, leading to two Stellar Award nominations and a Dove Award win. His arrangement of BTC's "The Battle Hymn of the Republic" was featured at the 2013 inauguration of President Barack Obama and simultaneously heard by over one billion people worldwide.

Mr. Webb wrote music and lyrics for Kenny Leon's production of *Much Ado About Nothing* (Shakespeare in the Park, The Public Theatre) *(also Music Supervisor/Incidental Music)*. His writing can also be heard on the hit TV series *Empire* (Fox), Netflix film *Juanita* (starring Alfre Woodard), recording projects and original musicals, including the new South African musical *WiLDFLOWER* (currently in development with NBT/Apollo Theatre).

Mr. Webb received a 2019 Special Tony Award for his "outstanding arrangements" in Tarell Alvin McCraney's breathtaking play *Choir Boy* (MTC). He is also a Drama Desk winner for Outstanding Original Music.

He served as Musical Director of the gorgeous Tony-, Emmy-, and Grammy-winning 2016 Broadway revival of *The Color Purple*, directed by John Doyle and based on the timeless novel by Alice Walker. Mr. Webb is now currently Music Director/ Arranger for Cynthia Erivo, who won a 2016 Tony Award as Celie in the Broadway revival.

Other credits include Associate Production Music Supervisor for *The Greatest Showman* (20th Century Fox); Musical Director and Arranger/Adaptor for Disney's *Frozen: Live at the Hyperion* (Anaheim, CA); and Associate Musical Director of Broadway shows including Berry Gordy's *Motown: The Musical*, Alan Menken's *Leap of Faith* and Jeanine Tesori's *Violet (also Additional Arrangements)*.

Mr. Webb has appeared as a pianist onstage with Dame Shirley Bassey, Michael Bolton, Cece Winans, and Chaka Khan. He has conducted live and recording orchestras from New York to LA, including internationally acclaimed pianist Lang Lang's 2016 love letter to NYC, *New York Rhapsody* (PBS), which featured performances by Rufus Wainwright, Regina Spektor, and Suzanne Vega.

**So where did it all start for you? Was it music or theatre first?**

No question, it was music first. I started playing piano when I was four. I studied classical piano, and I started working for churches when I was nine. So everything was very musical while I was growing up. Theatre didn't really enter my life until high school. There was a production of a small show that I think was called *Something In The Air*, or *Feels Like Tomorrow*. A really obscure show that we ended up doing. I ended up music directing and, by that point, I had been in the band at school and had a relationship with the teachers and they knew me as a musician, so they trusted me to music direct. And I remember, one of my distinct memories is, I must have been so excited to be in that environment that I remember the teacher just telling me to stop playing. Just stop playing. Because I guess in between every single thing I was just excited to do my thing!

**My high school teacher used to call that "noodling". [*Laughter.*]**

So I was always hungry to express myself, I guess. And, from that production, I don't think I touched theatre again until I started writing it. I wrote a piece that had a couple of readings. And, as a reward for one of the readings, the guy who was producing got me tickets to see *The Color Purple*. A couple of weeks before that play, I had a really terrible audition for Joseph Joubert where he was very encouraging, and when I went to see *The Color Purple* a few months after I'd auditioned for him and not gotten the gig, he asked me just in a text message, "Hey, would you ever be interested in playing for *The Color Purple*?" And I was like, "You know, it's very strange. I'm in the audience right now watching the show." And so, I ended up meeting him at intermission, and that's when my actual theatrical career got started.

**Did you think you were going to be a musical theatre composer or did you just like to write music?**

I definitely always wrote music. I was writing music in church, in any way that I could create something that people could then sing or perform. I really jumped at that. And when I discovered that theatre was another outlet that you can have, where you can create beginning, middle, and end journeys for characters, I just loved that. It was just an extension of what I'd already been doing in the pop world and the church world.

**Did you see a lot of theatre growing up?**

We would go on school trips to see theatre. I remember seeing *Damn Yankees* when I was young. I remember seeing *Miss Saigon*. But, outside of that, we didn't have a whole lot of exposure to theatre. Those few times when I was exposed to it, I identified it as something that I wanted to be a part of. And I just waited for the opportunity to do it. Then, finally, it presented itself when Joseph was like, "Hey, climb on board."

**Are you from New York originally?**

I'm from New Jersey originally. About an hour south of New York.

**What was that transition like from New Jersey to New York?**

Well, I think for those of us who are creative and live just outside of New York, we spend our childhood staring at New York and wondering when. When I was ever going to make it in. I have an aunt who still lives in New York who was a talent agent. And so I had a little bit of a connection, and a little bit of insight. When the opportunity started coming for me to actually land physically in New York, whether it was for pleasure or for work, it just fueled my desire more and more to get in. And finally I did.

**You mentioned Joseph [Joubert]. Of course, everybody is a mentor in a way, but certainly there are people who you came across that played significant roles in your journey.**

Well, like you said, we're all helping each other in some way. But there are some people who are laser focused on helping and really *mentoring* mentoring. Joseph was certainly that, and I'm sure he benefited from the relationship, because I would do his copy work and help in anything small. He had me beat on the playing, he had me beat on the history, he had me beat in so many ways that it was just such an inspiration to sit underneath his table and wait for gigs that he couldn't do to roll off. And that's kind of how I ended up building a career. Joseph was really the main one. There were a lot of people who poured into me in different ways. But Joseph was definitely the main one who helped me feel really safe about walking into such an unsure career path.

**As an artist of color, when you're navigating the industry and looking at this as a community, but also trying to find your community as well, how do you find your Black family on Broadway? How did you find your way into that?**

Well, I think that there's a certain shorthand and a certain understanding that those of us who kind of come from the same general place find a safety. I know I talk about safety a lot, but safety is so important in the creative process. Even when you're creating something, you want to be able to just give all of yourself and not have to worry about whether or not something terrible is going to happen to you as a result of it. So, identifying mentors who I could look at and say, "Oh, Joseph is a person of color, who was a pianist, trained classically. I have all those things in common," so I could look at his experience and look a little bit into what my future might be. But then, at the same time, look at his history, and feel the security and trust in him to lead me.

**So that brings us to *The Color Purple*. You're sitting in the audience, you have that moment, you connect. What starts rolling from there?**

Well, I had never sat in a Broadway pit before. I didn't know what any of that stuff was. And so he was very good about inviting me and explaining the whole thing as you do to someone who's brand new to it. And my whole thing is I like to play. I like to have a good time. I like to contribute something that I feel like maybe somebody else can't contribute. And that's how I approached going into work on *The Color Purple*. It was really just something like when you start auditing those shows and you sit in a Broadway pit. It's almost like that's when your audition starts. That's your first foot in the door and people start evaluating you for what you bring to the table and how chill you are and how reliable you're going to be.

**It absolutely is! Right from the first moment!**

I approached it with excitement, with enthusiasm, and with a feeling that I belonged. When I walked in, I felt like I was home, in a way. And with *The Color Purple* first production that had LaChanze, and subsequently Fantasia, the band had a prop table with toys and ladders and all that kind of craziness. And they would actually play a game and almost act out the show underneath the stage as the show was happening above the stage, which for me told me, oh, these are my people. And I guess when you're a sub you're supposed to play nice and be on your best behavior. I was like, I want that, I want that doll, I want the ladder, I want to say these lines. And, of course, I was on my best behavior at the beginning. But I tried to make it clear that I was here to play too. I wanted to have a good time. And I didn't want to be the guest that was coming in. I just wanted to get in the car. And I think that intersected with my ability to actually do the job. They began to trust me more and more. And, eventually, I ended up conducting that production of *The Color Purple*. So, that was my foot into theatre. And it was a beautiful production with a beautiful group of people that were doing it. That was my first show that I played and the full circle moment was when I music directed the revival.

**That's so fun. We all remember that first experience of being in the pit and auditing and encountering this idea that you have to be professional but also be creative and playful. And that those two worlds can exist simultaneously!**

It's the only way I like to work actually. As I'm getting older and I have more opportunities to pick and choose the gigs that I want and who I get to work with, I really only want to work with people who want to have a good time. That's where the magic is. Stuck is the wrong word but, if we're going to be in this room together eight shows a week for eight hours a day for six days a week while we're building it, we got to have a good time. We got to have fun. I've been in Broadway pits where it's been, "you get in here and you better do this." That's why I'm so thankful for Linda Twine. So thankful for Joseph and Shelton Becton who, if they weren't conscious of it, that at least on a subconscious level they were aware that element of fun got the best out of your people. That is something that I've tried to carry into everything that I've done.

**So that full circle moment with *The Color Purple*. You were asked to do the revival. Obviously the first production was so groundbreaking as far as our industry is concerned, and then it all comes full circle. How did that call come?**

I had decided not to associate music direct anymore. As I've gone through my career I've said, okay, I'm not going to be the rehearsal pianist anymore. I should be, at least, doing something in this room where I have some kind of say. And you have to keep saying no in order for them to give you the next thing. So, I was at the point where I was not going to associate music direct anymore. And, right after I decided that, Alan Menken's people called and they were doing *A Bronx Tale* and wanted me to associate, and I had to say no to that. I just hung up and cried. [*Laughter.*] But then they were doing a Bob Marley musical in Baltimore. And so I ended up booking that as music director. I had never gone out of town before to do a show and never really wanted to. But I was like, you know,

I'm going to go to Baltimore for these couple of months, what seemed like an eternity. And, while I was there, I found out that they were going to be looking to staff up *The Color Purple*. I don't remember who I heard it from; I would imagine it was from Joseph because he's all up in there. And so I met with the music supervisor who had already done it in the UK. She was coming into New York. I don't like to really broadcast what I'm doing before I do it so I didn't tell anybody what was happening. But I quietly got on a train on my off day at *Marley* and got up to New York, and I went and met with Cathy [Catherine] Jayes, and had an awesome meeting. They brought me on, and I got to meet John [Doyle] and that alone was an educational and life changing experience. What I learned from him, I have 100 percent taken into the things that I've done.

**What was that transition like in terms of going back to that material from ten years ago? Was it very different?**

Well, I worked in the church for a long time. And so I have a certain understanding of what music can do emotionally. I've seen music get the most mileage when it's emotional, when there's a heavy lean on the emotional aspect of it. The revival of *The Color Purple,* I think, was the initial production but with a heavy lean on the emotion. And so we stripped everything down. I was in an audition once where John said to somebody who was auditioning, "acting is not what you put on, it's what you take off." And so, I feel what the revival did was take off a lot of the putting on that the initial production did. And the putting on of the initial production was totally justified, because I would assume they endeavored to create a big Broadway musical for this incredible story that had never been told before on Broadway. But the revival was an attempt to distill it down to what was really going to touch people. To the point where there were almost no costumes, there was almost no choreography. You didn't see the band: they were hidden underneath the stage. It read like a play. Which I really feel helped people to focus on what Alice Walker had initially intended. And I want to say this is a true memory and, if it's not, then someone's going to correct me, but I feel like Alice Walker said that this was the closest to her book. That, out of all the ways that the story has manifested, that our version was the closest that ever came to the book. And I hope that's the case. Because, one: everything she says I just want to devour; and two: what a beautiful testimony to what John was able to do with the story that had already been presented.

**That's incredible. How has the journey been for you in terms of your church life coinciding as a theatre musician and your philosophy of healing and helping?**

I think anything that helps creative people open up their hearts and express themselves in some genuine way is an advantage. The church has been that for me. It not only, of course, developed me spiritually and caused me to look at my relationship to the world in a spiritual way, but caused me to look at my role in the church as a musician. Because, for me, the purpose of music is to affect people in some way. We can choose to affect people negatively; we can choose to affect people positively. Working in the church has been very largely a positive, affecting experience, and it's been incredible seeing people go from hurt to healed almost literally right in front of me. It almost creates a certain responsibility, where you realize, okay, I have this thing in my hand that's actually really powerful. And so what am I going to do with it? Now, in my own personal journey, I've had to look at if I'm putting positive energy into the world. Am I putting negative energy into the world? Why am I reacting to this thing in this way? Where am I coming from? How are all these things manifesting and why? I'm trying to say that the journey has been a conscious effort to make sure that I'm doing unto others as I would want done to myself. That's kind of the gist of it. So, as a journey, it's kind of simple in that every time you come into one of these rehearsal rooms or creative meetings, it's about bringing your best and thinking, okay, this choice that I'm about to make, is it going to make somebody's life better? Or am I going to get my kicks by making somebody's life worse? Like, why do you do that?

**Do you have any interest in creating musicals and creating a legacy in that way or do you like to focus on creating music?**

I think, overall, the philosophy that I use, and I say this in almost every negotiation that I go into, is I'm interested. Yes. And then we go in and get our titles and whatever we need for our careers and move forward. And then throw all that away, and know that we walked into this room, where none of us really know what it is and none of us know what it's supposed to be.

**Amen.**

And so approaching it with that type of humility to say, "let's find out what this is together." Which is why it's so important to hire the right

Zhailon Levingston

Baayork Lee

Beverly Jenkins

Linda Twine

Stafford Arima

Alex Lacamoire

Jason Michael Webb

Schele Williams

Kimberley Rampersad

Rick Sordelet

Masi Asare

people, because people have to approach it with that. Otherwise, the whole thing just kind of falls apart. As an artist, I would broaden whatever role or category I'm putting myself into "storyteller". I don't limit myself to theatre. I also think about what are the things that aren't TV, film, and theatre that we can tell stories by. I'm interested in that and don't want to keep myself away from that. I always look for the truth of whatever is either happening in the moment, or what's happening in that character. I just always want to look for whatever the truth is. And because that requirement isn't anything specifically musical, or specifically artistic even, anything can grow out of it. I may not be speaking scientifically correctly about this at all, but it's almost like a stem cell. Where all you have is the thing that makes anything else grow. And, as long as you're working from a stem cell place, then you can grow an ear, you can grow a foot, you can grow hair, anything can grow out of it. As long as you're open to being the scientist who's got to find what it's supposed to be at that moment. That's kind of how I approach it.

**Speaking about your career and how much you've done between composing, MDing, supervising, directing, is there a position in which you walk into a room and you really love it or is it all equal across the board?**

I'm really good for being really excited, and happy to share, and I love being in a room full of that. So there are times where I walk in, and I'll say, "oh, you guys, I have this great idea. We should X, Y, and Z." And then we'll start to build an idea around that. Nine times out of ten, though, it's just walking in and letting content dictate form. It's like you have to walk in to see what it is and let it tell you. Because any creative process is just a series of ideas. It's a bunch of people who feel comfortable enough to vomit out every crazy, silly idea that they have. And that we can all look at it and say, okay, not this one, not these, these don't work, but these are really cool. Let's put these over and look at them later and see how they strike us. That's how I think the best things are created.

**With working on *The Last Five Years* during the shutdown, what was the moment and journey of becoming both the director and MD for that production?**

Well, I'll say that whether you're music directing or an audition pianist, they're all creative, collaborative positions and they just kind of manifest in different ways and they have different levels of power. I always felt like a director when I was playing rehearsal piano and wanted to be able to contribute in that way. It wasn't, you know, power, power, power, I need to be able to run this room. It's no, I have something to say. I think that is valuable. And I would love to be able to share it and I don't think that ever ends. None of us ever grow up, none of us ever figure out really what's going on. That desire never really goes away. So, when I was initially approached about music directing *The Last Five Years*, which is a show whose music I've always loved, when I heard who was doing it, and under what circumstances they were doing it, I signed on immediately for that. And there was another director attached, who ended up getting another awesome gig, so they started looking for other directors. And I said, I think I have something to say. And they really graciously allowed me. They'd never seen any of the work that I've done behind the scenes, so they really took a shot. And I even had director ideas when they were just letting me be musical director. As the musical director I was saying, "we should have the musicians in the house and they have to be interacting, et cetera." That was even before we were talking about me directing, so I'd already kind of shared with them that I had a certain vision that I would love to just try out. They must have felt somewhat safe trusting me to do it because they did, and we ended up with something really, really beautiful.

**I think it speaks volumes to how, unfortunately, sometimes in the industry where people undervalue how much on a dramaturgical level the MD really has to be able to function in that world. Because if you don't understand dramatic intent, you can't create that arc.**

It's almost akin to an actor having lines and assigning the wrong subtext to the lines. It changes the entire meaning. And as a musical director, or even as a player in an orchestra, you have to realize the impact that you have as someone who is basically teaching the audience what they should be feeling in this moment. Or at least giving them the tools to feel it and then it's their choice to feel it or not.

**How has the pandemic affected the way that you've approached everything the last little while?**

Well, I think being locked up in the house for a year has really taught, I would imagine, all of us who we really are. It certainly taught me who I really am. Where before, I would say: if I had the time, I would do an album a month, I would write a song a day. Well, I had all that time and I haven't released any albums. And I certainly haven't written a song a day.

So it opened the window to myself to look inside and see what's really, really in there. And out of that has come a certain emotional place, from being cooped up in the house and not being able to hug and love all my people. That type of thing puts you in an emotional place, which I actually thought was really perfect for *The Last Five Years*, because it's such an emotionally rich show anyway. The entire company was in the same, almost wrought, emotional place that these two characters were in. We were all speaking the same language from top to bottom. And then everyone else joined in and kind of felt it. I think the emotional distress of the pandemic actually helped create something that would speak authentically to people who are watching it.

**Will we see more moments of directing where you're just titled as director?**

Yeah, I would love to head in that direction. I would love to direct more, but it's not a power grab. And not that I proved myself to be ultimately automatically trusted to tell every story. But I do look at the process that we went through to build *The Last Five Years* and the collection of awesome artists that came and gave generously. We were able to produce something that had not been presented in a certain way and may reach people in a way that it had not before. That's the work that I really endeavor to do. With the church, you change lives, and you really, again, help and heal people. It's work that has an effect that you can qualify. Almost quantify. So, yes, I want to direct more in an effort to be able to do that kind of work. To be able to really help people in that way. And to get stories told that may affect change in a way that we all really need.

I hope that because we've all learned new ways to work, and that there are these different ways to accomplish things that we were told before that we cannot accomplish. I probably would not have directed or been trusted to direct had it not been for this pandemic. But, now that we have, and now that we see what we can get out of it, then I would love the chance to do more of it in order to help someone else.

**Do you have any real hopes for things as we get back at it? And, with that, can you imagine some sort of vision in five or ten years of what our community looks like in terms of this moment?**

What I hope is a good analogy for what happens when we all get together creatively is: I feel when we are allowed to be in the room with our people and love on them, it will be without concern for getting sick. When we're able to do that, I know that I'm just going to throw myself on people. It's that type of enthusiasm that I feel like is going to happen. Creatively, I hope it's the same thing. I'm hoping over the next couple of years, because we've been apart, because we've had to retool the way that we collaborate, when we get back into those rooms, marrying those new ways of collaborating with the old ways of collaborating, that it will create this new enthusiasm to tell stories. With everything that's happening culturally right now, new voices are being allowed to tell those stories in ways that get a bigger platform. So I'm hoping that, in the next five or ten years, that we will be riding the wave of this enthusiasm from coming off of this Great Depression, basically. It's going to be the Roaring Twenties all over again. And we will arrive at a place that really reflects what this culture is, in all of its colors, and all its ages, and all the ways that it manifests. I hope that this pandemic helps us to appreciate that we've all got work to do. It's similar work to do, and that we should be doing it together.

**For someone reading this book, is there one thing that you could give to them as a note of encouragement or as some sort of imparting wisdom at this early part of their journey?**

I would say, whatever you apply to your life, in terms of making your life better, thinking ahead on how to make your life better, how to make yourself more healthy, take care of yourself: do the same thing creatively. Even from the beginning, and not to rely on others. You would never just rely on someone else to get you food every day. You would never just sit around and wait for someone to knock on your door and offer you a gig. That's just not how life works. So you have to take some type of initiative. The biggest leaps I've experienced in my career have come from moments when I've decided to take initiative to do something myself just because I wanted to do it. I worked for a big church in Queens for a long time, which had a large part in giving me the confidence to create. We would do the same Christmas production every year and one year I said, "would you guys let me do it? I'll write all new music, I'll create something that's different and special." And they, kind of like this *Last Five Years* thing where I had never done it before, said, "yeah, give it to Jason."

I spent a month, asked my friends, pulled in all kinds of favors, spent a month creating an album from start to finish, that ended up being performed that Christmas. And I went from being someone who came in and played and contributed to someone who could actually produce something from nothing. Once you do that, it puts you in a whole other category. And it works for musicians, it works for actors, it works for directors. You should have enough passion and drive to contribute something of your own. And if you don't, if you just ride it out, then it's probably just a job for you. And you're going to find out what your actual calling is. But if your calling is to create, you should have the passion and drive to do it. And it's actually going to help you. Growing up, I did not hear, "Create your own content, do your own thing." I stumbled on it. I did it and everybody said, "Oh Jason, we want you to—" and I was the same Jason who they were talking to six months ago, but now they know that I do this different thing.

So, my biggest encouragement would be: study your craft and don't give anybody excuses to say that you don't deserve it. Don't give anybody excuses. Hone your craft, be the best that you can at it, and then actually do something with it. Let's say that you are only an actor. But if you're only an actor, then you must have a director friend. You must have a writer friend. You must have somebody else that you can go and create some one-person show or one-person short film. You've got iPhones, they have good lenses on them. You can go in iMovie and edit. Create something for yourself and show people why you deserve tobe heard.

**Is there anything you're really excited about that's coming up?**

I'm really excited about winning my Oscar and my—no, I'm just kidding.

**[*Laughter.*] Add it to the shelf with the Tony and the Drama Desk.**

No, things are on the near horizon, but I'm most excited about whatever's coming that I can't see yet. I'm always excited about *that* stuff.

**That's a moment of inspiration, for all of us. Thank you, Jason!**

# SCHELE WILLIAMS

**Schele Williams** is a director committed to cultivating new musicals and devised work with authentic representation on stage and off. Profiled in *Variety*'s Top 10 Broadway to Watch, she is currently directing the upcoming Broadway revivals of *Aida* (Disney Theatrical Group) and *The Wiz* as well as the premieres of *Mandela the Musical* and *Indigo*, and co-directing *The Notebook* premiering at Chicago Shakespeare Theatre in Fall 2022. She will also be helming *Hidden Figures*, currently in development (Disney Theatrical Group). Schele has directed at regional theatres and festivals across the country and has a long history of work on Broadway in *Rent*, *Aida*, and *Motown: The Musical*. Passionate about pairing social justice with the arts, Schele is a founding member of Black Theatre United, an organization committed to dismantling systemic racism on our streets and stages. She has been a member of Broadway Inspirational Voices for over two decades and serves as Chairperson of the Board, and also serves on the board of Broadway Care Equity Fights AIDS. Schele is the author of the children's book *Your Legacy: A Bold Reclaiming of Our Enslaved History*, recipient of a 2022 Boston Globe-Horn Book honor.

**Did you always know you wanted to be in musicals? I know your life as a performer, of course, which is a big part of your journey to, your work now as a director. But was it always musicals? Or did you kind of find your way there?**

No, I grew up as a musician. I was a drummer. My dad's a professional drummer. And I played in the pit of shows in the high school and regional productions.

**That's very cool. And, am I correct—that your dad was the drummer for the Ohio Players?**

Yeah.

**That is dope as hell.**

Yeah, it is dope as hell. Yeah.

**It's amazing.**

He's awesome. Yeah.

**So cool. So music strictly?**

Yeah, I was, full on, you know. That was my journey. I had always sung in church and I had danced my whole life, mostly because I just had a bunch of energy and my parents just wanted to keep me busy. So I did a lot of dance classes but music was my thing. I was gonna go to college for music. And in my senior year they were doing *The Wiz*. And I auditioned for Dorothy. And I got it. And then I was like, oh no, I'm questioning my life choices. I had this really awkward conversation with my parents and I told them that I was going to turn down a music scholarship and go into theatre, which I had not studied at all. Unlike percussion, where I'd been taking private lessons since I was in the fifth grade. So I took a gap year from college and worked at the mall to pay for my acting lessons so that I could have a monologue and a song to audition for schools. It was bananas. And God bless my parents for letting me do it and not strong-arming me and saying, "no, you're going to this specific school". I really did have to hone my craft as much as I could.

I got a scholarship from AMDA, and then came to New York and began to pursue musical theatre as a major. It was so funny because I could talk about Stravinsky, but I couldn't talk Sondheim. I played in orchestras. I went to orchestra camp. I knew a whole other vocabulary of music. I thought I was going to be like the Black female Vic Firth in the London Philharmonic Orchestra playing xylophone proficiently. I just had a very different idea of my life. And suddenly I was trying to cram Hammerstein and Lerner and Loewe and Kurt Weill. I was like, who's that? And I'm around all these people in school and this was their lifeblood. So it was quite a learning curve for me.

**That's amazing. What was it like being in New York at that time? Since you'd already had exposure to arts and even in the community in Ohio, was it shocking?**

You know, I traveled a lot with my dad and his bands so I'd seen a lot of the country. I'd seen a very sheltered version of it. I was in nightclubs, I was in the dressing room, or backstage with my mother. I wasn't venturing out into the nightlife of the world. I was very, very sheltered in that regard. But when I came to New York for the first time, I actually came with my orchestra, the Dayton Philharmonic Youth Orchestra. And we played the first youth concert at Carnegie Hall. And a young trumpeter named Steve Reineke, who is now conductor of the [New York] Pops, was in the orchestra when we were friends in high school.

**Is he from Ohio as well?**

Yes, he is! I've known Steve since I was fifteen. So, I came to New York to play Carnegie Hall, which is bananas. And I fell in love with the city. I mean, there was something about it. I was like, oh, this is where I'm supposed to be. Dayton, Ohio never felt like it was the best place to be from, but I knew that I just kind of felt like I was like a fish out of water. I was the girl who dressed weird and walked too fast. And I got to New York and I was like, my people! Everything about it felt good. When I did graduate, and I got into AMDA a few years later, and it felt so great to be in New York. It's incredibly stimulating: the colors, the languages you hear walking down the street, the culture, the music you hear coming out of people's apartments. You're just immersed. The world gets bigger every day. You're sitting on the train, and you're like, oh, my gosh, my understanding of humanity has grown exponentially between 14th Street and 96th Street. I'm still in a mad love affair with New York City. It is my first love. I say to my husband, I love you so much, but oh my god, New York. So that's how I got to New York and got into theatre. That's a very long answer to a very short question.

**But it's such a testament to the multitude of journeys that exist to getting into what we do, right?**

And how everything I did makes everything that I do better. I read music; I understand how rhythm works. My love for orchestra was really helpful when you're doing musical theatre. Dancing all of my life, understanding movement, understanding how to tell a story with your body, singing for so many years. Those are all tools that, even though I'm not exercising them on a daily basis, certainly make me a better director.

**For me, the most symbiotic moments I've had in terms of working with directors have come where both of them studied music, could read music, and were musicians first. I always found that it was such a privilege because we just instantly spoke a similar language of not having to explain bars and how that factors into framing and rhythm. Do you still send to your musicality as a part of your work as a director as well?**

Yeah. I mean, I mostly direct musicals. And the music is the engine. I kind of don't understand it when people don't understand music. Because it's a learned skill. It's not like I was born with it. You can learn it. It's not impossible. So I'm deeply curious about all the ways music is functioning in a show. I think a lot about: it's a great song, is it in the right key? A lot of times, composers will compose, especially for women, that great power number. And she's belting C's and D's and F's. And I say, she's not in her power there. That's not her place of power. That's where you like to hear her. But that's actually not where she's the most powerful. So having those conversations and asking that woman, who's singing that song, where she feels for strength. And if that's what you're trying to convey, those are the notes that you need to be going for. Not what you think sounds exciting but how we are telling the story. Because music should be telling the story. And if you want a great thrill, go to an amusement park. Right? There are other ways to achieve that. But sometimes it can be a false climax. Because it's not truly telling the story in the moment. So I do think about music a lot. It's very hard for me to be in an audition and hear someone sing out of time. Time is a thing for me and someone will ask, what did you think of them? And I'm like, they were ahead of the beat. I couldn't hear them. That's the thing that I can't handle. A piano player who plays a little too fast. I'm like, stop. I literally stop breathing. So in that way, I'm fully hampered.

**It's interesting, I did my Master's thesis specifically in looking at music direction as dramaturgy, You do a great amount of work in terms of new stuff. And so I'm curious, do you consider yourself a dramaturg? Is that an approach to the work as a director as well?**

Yeah, for sure. But I try to think about the logic of everything. Could they do that? Have we established that this family actually makes enough money to do this? Does this line up with all of the things that we know about the characters that are on the page? Not the things that are in our head, but the things that made it to the page? So I think, as completely as I can, about the story, the logic of the story, the why of it. Why a certain character? Why are we thinking of this character a certain way? Is it our implicit biases? Are we really questioning ourselves and double checking ourselves at every turn? So I think very deeply.

I love to be on a piece really early on and be in discussions and be collaborative in the process. I really have such a passion for new shows. I do have a couple of revivals coming up. But even my revivals that I'm doing, I think, why this story? Why now? What is relevant about this moment and why is this the moment to tell the story? So I open them all up. And I'm very candid with producers, when they say, we want you to do this. And I say, okay, but I'm not going to rubber stamp what was. We have to really talk about why. If you want me, you have to be willing to crack this open. And that's okay if you don't and if they say, hey, we want what it was because it was a big fat hit so let's do that again. That's fantastic. That's just not for me. Somebody else has already done that. So I'm happy for that to happen and I'm happy for you to move on. But I want to approach everything with a newness. I want to think about not where we are but where we're going to be. By the time it hits the stage, I still want to be ahead of the audience. I love making art. I love thinking about it. I love conversations about it. And I love the challenge of being more than relevant. Being forward thinking.

**That's the only way we're ever going to bring in the true shift right?**

Yeah. And to do that, you actually have to be a historian. Right? Because you can't arrive somewhere and think that you've been here first. That may be new for you but for everybody else who's been reading books, we know that's already happened. You really do have to be a steward of history and look to see: when has this happened before? Is the most interesting thing about this story is that we keep perpetuating this narrative? Because we haven't found the best way to socialize these concepts in a way that is sticky for people to hold on to. I could get really heady about that.

**Certainly in terms of leadership and activating that leadership in the room and community, those are the sorts of questions we want our artistic leaders to be prodding and asking, right? Because otherwise, why even bother doing this work?**

Absolutely.

**So, you're in New York, and AMDA's done. What's the time between AMDA and *Rent* like? Was *Rent* the first big big one?**

So I did my first show at Queen's Theatre in the Park. I was very fortunate that while I was doing *They're Playing Our Song* there, I booked the *42nd Street* European tour. Which was magnificent. We opened in Rome and it was just magical. I did that tour for a while and then I did *Porgy and Bess* with the great Baayork Lee. Between the tours, I did *A Chorus Line* in New Jersey. And I met Baayork during the course of that. I was playing Maggie and she called me up and said, "Hey, I'm doing this tour of *Porgy and Bess* in Europe. I'd love for you to be a part of it." And I did it and it was extraordinary. The first and only opera I've ever done. It was magnificent for a musician to be around this giant orchestra with sixty voices. It was just incredible. Then I went back and I ended up doing *Tommy*. They did a production of *Tommy* in Germany. Michael Cerveris and Roger Bart came over and opened the show for the first year. So I had the most incredible time working with these unbelievable actors. The company was fantastic.

And then when I came back, I got the opportunity to audition for *Rent*. But my journey with *Rent* began when I was the merchandise gal in previews. I ended up getting the tour. I'll also say that, when I did *Tommy*, I was a swing. And I called Baayork, and I asked her, you know, how do you swing? Should I take the job? I don't know. And she was like, "okay, girlfriend, come on over, I'm going to tell you everything you need to know", and she taught me how to swing. When I got *Rent*, I was the dance captain. And I was like, "Baayork, I'm dance captain, what do I do?" And she's like, "okay, girlfriend, I'm gonna teach you how to build a book." And she taught me how to build a dance captain book. You know, she's amazing. And she said to me, a hand to God, she said, you do every single thing that I tell you and you will be setting companies of this show all over the world, just like I did with *A Chorus Line*. And, hand to God, that's exactly what happened. That is exactly what happened. So I made my Broadway debut in *Rent*. I did the show, first as a swing, and then I was Production Dance Supervisor, and then I ended up going into New York for a little while. And then *Aida*. In and out of there were lots of readings where I did a lot of original readings. I did about four workshops of *Wicked* and I saw lots of readings. A lot of shows that became Broadway shows, I was part of the early processes of those and so I had a really great time watching art grow and evolve even while I was doing my long standing shows.

**That's so lovely to bring into scope, which is always considering that everybody who works in your ecosystem and who you know. You just never know who you're going to be working with in a room, right?**

I mean, it's so beautiful. And it's so true. You know, I always think of everyone as family. When I am doing a show I'll say to the cast, one of the most important things when we get into the theatre is that you learn every single person's name. They deserve the dignity of you knowing their name. We're all making art together. You know your dresser's name, you know the person at the stage door's name, you know the person who's handing you props. You give them the dignity of learning that on day one, even if you have to write it down. I'm terrible with names. I have a clipboard with names written all over it and I study it. Oh, my gosh, when I'm on my way to the first day of rehearsal, and I cast everybody, I'm literally staring at a page on the train with their little pictures. It's not easy for me. But, I tell you, I can walk into the Lunt-Fontanne right now. I haven't been there in eight or nine years. And I know the bartender. I know the Stage Door person. I could walk into the Nederlander and it's like home. It's like, "Schele!" I could walk into the Palace Theatre and go, "Eddie! How you doing?" You know, that to me is a beautiful part of what we do. Because, if I'm missing my cousin's wedding, so is Eddie. What we do is hard. And there's so many sacrifices. And that day that you schlep in in the middle of a snowstorm. When you're like, oh, God, please, call it a week so we can all stay home. It's so cold, I don't want to get out in this slush. And you're making it in; and so did everybody else. What we do is hard. And it's beautiful. But the sacrifices that we make personally to create art I don't ever think has a bright enough light on it. And certainly in the last two years. The extraordinary risk that everyone all over the world took. In addition to our theatre makers who are aerosolizing all over each other, doing one of the most dangerous things that you can do in terms of a working activity. There's no way to do that with a mask on. And we show up for each other, and we love each other, and we support each other and it's beautiful.

**What was the moment that you realized that directing was it for you?**

The moment I realized I was too mouthy. I'd be like no, that's not it. That light cue should be later. I don't know why I'm crossing my arms. He should not cross on that line. I would say, no one will ever want to direct me again. I need to get to the other side of the table because I'm just going to start torturing any person who hires me.

**Nothing wrong with having an opinion!**

I remember being at understudy rehearsal and we had a star in one of the male roles. And he said, I don't know why I'm crossing there. They told me to cross there. And I said, your gut is right. That's a terrible place to cross. And he said, I should cross on that line. I'm like, of course you should. You should be. Yes, yes, just go with that. No one's gonna give you a note. They won't even notice. But your gut is right, follow that. So I was pretty clear that I was not one for taking orders.

**What have been some of the most rewarding moments for you in your career as a director that have been different from your work before as a performer?**

You know, they're tiny moments. As a director, I see pictures in my head. I get a lot of inspiration when I'm in the shower. A lot of times in production meetings I'd say, "Well, I was in the shower and I realized we should move the song." But it's really incredible to go from a picture in my brain to seeing it in rehearsal, or I see it on stage and it is as magical as my imagination. Equally satisfying for me is when I imagine something in my brain so perfectly and then an actor on stage does something different that is infinitely better than what I imagined. Then I know that, not only have I cast the right person, but the art is growing beyond my imagination, which is the best thing ever.

**Is there a different sense of purpose for you and immediacy in this moment now that the industry does have an eye on really making sure that voices that weren't heard before are heard now? Do you think about that a lot?**

Yeah, there's two things. The immediacy for me is having the deep conversations, right? It's very easy for someone to have a knee-jerk reaction to say, oh my gosh, this event happened. We should all get canned goods and send over supplies. Right now, we're watching everything happen in Ukraine. And there's lots of lists of things that people are sending. And that's wonderful. And it's noble and it's needed. But without a deeper understanding of what is actually going on, you can't go beyond your shopping list to be effective for the long term. Right? So I'm not looking for people to say, give me a list so I can fulfill that and say, I've checked the box, I've done the good thing, and I'm moving on. I want to have the deep conversations with people about how we got here. What the cause and effect is of the decisions that have been made, how it has changed the art, the impact the art has on the greater public. The impact it has on the lives and deaths of people, and the responsibility that we as an industry have to take that on. Because when you then say, no, later on, or it doesn't matter, I want you to be fully aware that this is no longer a decision you're making out of ignorance. You are contributing to the problem or you are contributing to the solution.

So I'm not interested in a quick answer and a knee-jerk reaction. I'm interested in sitting in a very uncomfortable place while you learn. Which is incredibly humbling for people who have "known" everything for a very long period of time. It was very humbling to become a parent at thirty-nine years old. Because, at that point, I was good at a few things. Pretty good. I had a good career. I had some things under my belt. I've been married for a few years, I felt very good about myself. I had a child. And suddenly I was like, I know nothing. I don't know anything at all. None of the books were right. It was so humbling. It was humiliating. It still is. It's one of those things where you realize there are times in your life that you have to surrender to grow. So I do think that there is an immediacy to having the conversations while the ears are open. I do think there is an immediacy to, with grace, check the mistakes so that we are acknowledging them in real time. You know, much like a private teacher when you play your solo, and they say, oh, you missed that, you missed that rest. You blew right through that and that's a tied note. Those kinds of things, right? Make the music better. It's the same thing to me. We're actually on this journey to make this better.

But what I'm very clear about, because I get a lot of offers for a lot of projects, is I would ask them "why me?" Because if you're not choosing me because you want my unique voice, then no. I don't want to have a conversation just because you want to talk to a Black person. You can just flip open the phonebook and find a Black person. I want to be hired because you understand, as an artist, what I have to offer to this piece. And if you're not interested in doing that little bit of homework, then I have no interest in knowing you either. I'm not going to go on the deep dive because I've never had the luxury of walking into a room and not knowing every single thing about the person I was talking with. I knew where they went to college, I know where they live because that is assumed. So, if they're not doing the same on me, when I sit down with someone and they ask, you wrote a book? I'm like, yeah this is over. This is going to be the shortest conversation ever. So it's been a really incredible year and a half, coming up on two years, because there are conversations that I never imagined would happen in my lifetime. Which is a sad and terrible thing to say out loud. And it has been exhausting. But I am grateful that we are recognizing and acknowledging that we have to do better, that the art has to be better, the people have to be better, the work environments have to be better. So I feel very, very good about that. I have a lot of hope.

**Did you have the mentorship of a Black director that showed you how you see yourself or where you see a version of what you could be in the industry?**

Nope. Not at all.

**How did that affect you in terms of how you got to this point?**

It's so interesting. I never assumed that I would. It's horrifying. You know, I didn't see Black women directors growing up. I didn't see them. None of my professors in college were Black women. There were very few Black women who were leads in shows. So I wasn't thinking in the upper echelons of theatre that there would be Black women. As a woman of color, I did have Baayork Lee as an incredible mentor. When I worked on *Rent*, Marlies Yearby was a wonderful mentor. She's a choreographer and a wonderful mentor. I've always had mentors in my life and I still have mentors. I will always, as long as I'm breathing, be seeking the counsel of my elders to know more and be better. I always have three or four mentors and I pick up the phone no matter what. Sometimes I have to be aware of what time zones they're on but, if something comes down, I'm going to talk it out with them. So that's very real for me, but, still to this day, I don't have Black women mentors. I have Black women in my life because of Black Theatre United that I have revered for a long time. And I'm now in deep and wonderful conversations with them about everything from art to motherhood to the business, and that has been a saving grace for me that it has brought us together.

**I know that you're a proud mom.**

My kid just came home from school. I don't know if you can hear them but I hear them in the stairs right now.

**How does that affect your creation and your existence as an artist?**

When I became a mom, I became a better listener. So I think of it as my director superpower. The way I describe it is, it's the things I never really knew how to do until I became a mom. When you have a child, and before they are verbal, you're trying to figure out everything from a cry. You ask, is that a wet cry? Is that an "I'm hungry" cry? Is that an "I need to burp" cry? And your ear gets real, real good. You're like, oh, change the diaper. You're suddenly able to distinguish a "wah". It's such a silly thing, right? So for me, when I sit in rehearsal, I will often close my eyes and listen to a scene and I'll say, "you're uncomfortable with that line and you don't believe it. I can hear it in your voice, that there's something. What's going on in this moment?" I can hear when someone is in that place, when they're connected, when they understand their intention. And, for people who are not in the first twelve rows, it's odd, because the whole show for them is what they hear. There's blobs on stage in costumes. They're not seeing faces. The show for them is a radio play with set and costumes, right? So hearing, understanding, learning how to listen. And understanding how important our physical storytelling is is vital for people who are not in the first twelve rows. They still deserve to hear a fully connected journey and your face cannot do all the work. So I feel like being a parent made me infinitely more sensitive to the nuance of human behavior, but certainly a much, much better listener than I've ever been.

**What advice would you give young, upcoming artists and young professionals who want to do the same thing? Who are looking at the next five years and wondering what the industry is going to look like and how it's going to shift or not?**

You know, when I came out of school in 1990, I didn't see myself. LaChanze was doing *Once on This Island*. So I saw her and that was my first little bit of hope. I'd seen Stephanie Mills in *The Wiz* in the late 70s. Two people are not defining for your entire career life choice, right? When I came out of school, it was all the tall girl shows. It was *Will Rogers Follies*. You had to be like 5'8" or taller and I'm 5'5", so there was already a barrier of entry beyond my brown skin to get into any of these shows. But what I knew it was what I wanted to do. And I've had a number of students I've spoken with, students at universities who are graduating and saying, will there be an industry for me? I never thought about that when I didn't see myself. I was like, I'm going to be there. And I'm going to take up space. And so I don't think about what everyone else is doing around me. I just do it. When I wanted to be a director, I wasn't looking around and saying, "what other Black women do I know? I just hung my own sign. I was like Lucy in Charlie Brown. The doctor's in. I just want to do it. I didn't have an agent until a couple years ago. I've never been afraid of the hustle. I've always had a hustle. All through the pandemic I was doing 15,000 things. I've never been afraid of work. When I was in school, I went to dance lessons. I cleaned the bathrooms at Broadway Dance Centre so I could get the lessons. The work has never made me nervous. I sold T-shirts at a Broadway show because that was getting me closer to a Broadway show. I wanted to be in it. I wanted to be around it. I couldn't afford to see it. Now they're paying me and I get to sit there and watch the show every night. And at intermission I sell T-shirts and hats. What could be better? So I've never looked for someone to make a space for me. I've always found a space. And I man-sprawl. I'm the dude on the train that just spreads his legs and is like, Ha ha! Now I've got a little more space, you know? And then, eventually, I have my own seat. And it has been much slower than my peers. I've watched people that came up with me go on and have many, many, many more shows to their credit than I do. But I've had a very joyful journey. And I love the art that I've made. And some of it's been picked up and some of it hasn't. But there's no other way that I'd want to do it.

**Schele, remarkable. Thank you so much. Is there anything else you want to add?**

I could talk about theatre all day. I love talking about theatre. You know, I love it so much. I've spent the last thirty years of my life doing it. I switched my whole world around to do it. So I love it. You know, my husband was saying that in a few years he can imagine retiring. I say, I'll never retire. If this is the thing that brings me so much joy, why would I ever not want to do it? That's where my heart is. I will always, always, always be making theatre.

**Keep on pushing, as the song goes.**

# KIMBERLEY RAMPERSAD

 **Kimberley Rampersad** is a Canadian theatre artist, born and raised in Winnipeg, Manitoba, Treaty 1. As an actor, she has appeared in various theatres across Canada including Mirvish, RMTC, Stratford, and Shaw. She is a recipient of a Maud Whitmore Scholarship (Charlottetown Festival), a Guthrie Award (Stratford Festival), and was inducted into Rainbow Stage's Wall of Fame as a performer in 2018.

She was engaged as the associate choreographer for *Hairspray— The Musical* (NETworks) for the North American and Asian tours for four seasons. Her work as a choreographer was recognized in 2017 with two Dora nominations for *Passing Strange* (Musical Stage/Obsidian) and *Seussical—the Musical* (YPT) respectively, and an Evie Award in 2019 for *Matilda—The Musical* (Royal MTC/Citadel/Arts Club). As a director, Kimberley was featured in the *New York Times* in July 2019 for directing her full-length production of *Man and Superman* at the Shaw Festival. Other directing credits include *Routes* (MTYP), *hang* (with Philip Akin, Obsidian), *How Black Mothers Say I Love You* (GCTC) (2018 Prize Rideau Award—Outstanding Production) and *The Color Purple* (Neptune and Citadel/Royal MTC) which received Sterling and Merritt Awards for Outstanding Direction and Production among others. She is the recipient of the 2017 Gina Wilkinson Prize for an emerging female director (Ontario Arts Foundation.)

Beyond the stage: Kimberley completed her dance teacher certification through, and was on faculty with the Royal Winnipeg Ballet School for four years; she was a full-time dance clinician with the Winnipeg School Division for six years, including co-contributing to writing the dance curriculum for the Province of Manitoba's Department of Education; and she holds a Bachelor of Arts degree, majoring in Political Science, from the University of Manitoba.

She is currently the Associate Artistic Director of the Shaw Festival in Niagara-on-the-Lake, Ontario.

**So where did the road start? When did you realize that it might be the theatre for life?**

I can't remember it clearly, but I remember senses and feelings of it. There were some really important moments. There's this theatre called Rainbow Stage. I was already dancing and it was already my love. Dancing is my first love. It always will be. This theatre called Rainbow stage is the largest outdoor stage in Canada. We did *Annie* when I was ten. And I've never looked back.

**What age did you start dancing at?**

I think I was five. It's always been around. I can't imagine a moment where I didn't know what I wanted to do. It was just this cumulative effect of experiences that added to that yes, this is your path. Yes, this is what you're supposed to do. So it literally is a series of "yes, and" from the universe.

**That's very divine.**

I hope so. In a very practical way though so that people feel like they have a calling.

**That's beautiful.**

I hope the theatre is my calling. I hope that it's evident in the way that I do my work in a good way. That people are like, yeah, this is what she's supposed to do because she leaves more good in her wake than anything else.

**Was there a certain dance style that you leaned towards?**

Ballet was my first in. Absolutely. It was my first love. I loved ballet and I did very well in ballet but my body just has limitations. You could certainly work to create more, but I was discovering what my limitations are, at about ten or eleven, and I was like, "oh, okay, this is what's happening." Then when I discovered musical theatre, that's when *Annie* happened. Jazz and tap, I liked those a lot, but they came easily even more so because that's what musical theatre was. And there wasn't as much ballet being featured in the musical theatre that I was starting to learn about. There was a lot of jazz and tap. So then I said, well, musical theatre is the thing that I'd like to do because it lets me sing and dance and act. So, I get to take the ballet and the jazz and the tap and the modern that I'm doing and then I get to sing and act? Right, I'll see you on the stage.

There's something really beautiful in that. As artists, we're trained to be afraid of our shortcomings and say, maybe that's not in my body, or maybe that doesn't rest with me, versus embracing that feeling that this is directing me to where I am meant to be. There is that ability to use that as we discover, right?

I think that I was also very fortunate that as I was starting to understand what my limitations in ballet were, it was superseded by my love for musical theatre. And seeing that there were more styles involved and then realizing that I actually had an even stronger facility for jazz and tap. It was almost as if the heartbreak of not being able to pursue a classical dance was superseded by this new thing. This other love took over. So the heartbreak wasn't as tremendous. So that's just divine, because I'm sure I could have been on the floor like any other person who just learns one thing before discovering the other. Those moments happening on top of one another also kept me in love with ballet. Maybe ballet didn't love me back in a certain way. But it certainly didn't stop me from loving ballet. So, that was important too because ballet is such a foundational dance.

**Did you know for post-secondary studies that musical theatre or theatre was going to be it? What were your thoughts when you started your programme on the first day of university?**

Well, that was really hard because I had to do everything on my own as my parents didn't support me going into theatre. Not at all. My parents put my sister and myself in dance and then supported us through all of our artistic practices and development to be well rounded humans. To be graceful, to excel in those things, but certainly not to pursue them as a livelihood. So when I went to university, I was filled with rage as I did my honours political science degree. I was filled with rage. You've never seen an angrier child who was given the opportunity to go to university. I had to do everything on the side. So I went to dance class every day, I went to my singing classes twice a week, I went to my theatre classes, but I did them all right alongside. So I'd go to university in the day and then I go to Kimmy University at night.

**It's interesting that that journey is so common, right? And especially with parents and families of color. That's what we do. It's not out of a disinterest in the arts, it's out of knowing what it takes for your child to survive in the world and wanting to, as best as possible, set that up from the get go.**

My parents said, we can't afford. You can't afford. We don't have enough generational wealth. We do not have these things so that you can afford to go through the ups and downs of being an artist. My parents aren't delusional. They said, look at you, Kimberley, look at the parts they're asking you to play. Look at this, look at that. We don't really care for you to go and train and then to play the parts of prostitutes and maids. And that's what it looks like this industry is filled with for you right now. So only now I can be like, okay, Mum and Dad, I'll give you that. I can be a little more, I hope, empathetic and understanding of why it is. I do understand that they said, we didn't come to this country for that. Here's some choices for you: doctor, lawyer, and we might settle for a teacher.

**And now, with everything that you're done and that you're doing, they couldn't be prouder. But the road is long, and it's hard to see to the end of it at the start.**

But then it makes every step on that journey more meaningful, because you are being so thoughtful and, for me too, in times being so defiant. Every step had so much meaning because it was in defiance of my family, it was towards my calling and the duality of feeling that both of those things existed in the same space. I thought, how could something that feels like a calling to me be in defiance of my family. But, this is life.

**And you speak about your parents and your family being such a part of that journey and having that generational grounding and the arrival to Canada from Trinidad, which of course, people may not be familiar with generationally. What do you think about all that, especially now as an artist and thinking about that movement that your parents had?**

I think we all just have different waters. And mine: we're more emotional than physical. I think about my parents' ancestors and our elders that came from India, that came from the continent of Africa. And they traveled over these big waters to get to Trinidad where my parents happened to meet. Then they traveled over big waters to come to Treaty One to Winnipeg. And then I traveled different waters. My parents and so many generations traveled big waters physically and obviously emotionally, being torn from their people and all these different things. And mine was a pivot where it was more emotional than over land. Which, in a crazy way, that is my inheritance for still being here, because they made sure that I'm here. So what does success look like in adversity? It means that all of a sudden, my waters changed from something physical to something emotional, where I pulled away in a different way to declare my sovereignty over myself with relationship to them. Understanding that, unfortunately, I was being defiant, but not doing it maliciously because I wanted to upset them: because I knew that this was who I was.

**How did you feel when you were now in that performing world, as a performer primarily?**

It was beautiful. I loved the stage because it felt like such a conversation with everyone. I'm going to cry about it. I've never been happier. Yeah. I've never been happier than when I'm on stage. Even telling terrible stories; such a delight in doing that for people and with people. I think I was in Grade Three. And we had a little musical we did at school. And it was *Goldilocks and the Three Bears*. And everybody had to audition and I auditioned for Goldilocks. And I got it. Ms. McCrory was like, Kimberley, you've got the part. But you have to imagine, here I am in North Kildonan, which is a very predominantly white Mennonite suburb in Winnipeg, Manitoba, Canada. And I got to play Goldilocks. And, I remember, my mom was like, well, that sounds very nice. So we woke up and we put my hair in ringlets and my parents took the morning off from work so they could come to the assembly. And my parents didn't tell me at the time because they were not going to weigh me down with anything other than the joy in the moment, but they could hear parents and people tittering, how was she playing Goldilocks, and this and that. But all I could remember from that was that my teacher thought that I was the most prepared and the best person to play Goldilocks. And they didn't put a blonde wig on my head. They were just like, just imagine. It's a feeling. What else can gold mean? Just put her hair in ringlets and she's gonna sing the song. But it's amazing, because that one action of Ms. McCrory defined how I decided that I would be treated or the pursuit of it in every casting room. I decided that needed to be the start of the pattern. Anyways, I love the stage. I just had to throw in the Ms. McCrory story because when people talk about what it is to see somebody, there was somebody who saw me and saw how a part was interpreted in the past, and did not feel bound to cast it that way. And that was something that other people would have said, well, sure, her. But here's a blonde wig. Ms. McCrory said, she is Goldilocks because we said so. Everyone on stage will believe it.

**And that's the true belief it takes in the purity of storytelling. That's gonna be a very important story for other young girls everywhere who are going to be thinking the same thing.**

And for teachers to know how much power they have. How much power a teacher and educator has that Ms. McCrory decided for me and helped me decide how I should be seen for the rest of my life as an artist in Grade Three.

**Did you ever connect with her afterwards?**

No, and she passed away. I wish I could have told her.

**Somewhere along the line, it started to move to helping to lead others through that and loving it as well. Was it gradual or was there a moment where you thought about being a choreographer or director?**

I think it was gradual. Before I started playing secondaries or leads, I spent a lot of time in the ensemble. Which was fine because I love the ensemble and I love dancing my face off, and that's what some of us do. But, because I spent so much time in the ensemble, I spent a lot of time as dance captain. I'd be picked for dance captain a lot. Before I had a choreographer's and a director's résumé, I had the ensemble and the artist résumé and I had lots of dance captain in my ensemble roles. So I think maybe that's where a little bit more of leadership started because you're there to help people. You're there to share information. You're there to give positive feedback about things. You're there to give notes and or corrections that need to be applied. And you want them to be applied. So what is that way of communication and the manner in which you can communicate it where you are not disrespecting someone? Some people are sensitive but you still need to get them to do the note. You don't want to come and give it to them three times because you're circling around the drain. So how do you give the notes? Be respectful, be mindful of the personality and the person who needs to receive it. Is that something that should happen in front of people? Is that something that's really small over your shoulder as you're signing in over the cardboard? Does that need to be a formal note? Whatever it was, it was me learning about all those things.

**It's such a fine balance, isn't it?**

It is because there's an art to it. And you want every note to be given once and to be applied correctly. And you want efficiency because they're not paying you enough to give the notes more than once. Oh, my God, as dance captain, you do it for the love. You do it for the kind of trajectory if you see it. You do it for many things but, certainly when I've done it, I certainly was not getting paid for it.

**I'm doing this work with this new group, Musicians United for Social Equity, and everyone's asking, well, how do we get people here? What do we do? And not underestimating the idea of putting value into the training. Not just doing the training, but that not all of us can do the training and afford to not be paid for it in the same way.**

This is it. So then what is the obvious social advantage of the people who can afford to not get paid? The absolute systemic inequities that are built in this idea of free labour for the experience. But I digress, it started with dance captaining, I think. And choreography is something that I've always loved. So, choreography felt like a kind of natural progression. I think it was a mix of being in the room as an ensemble dancer and a lot of times people ignore you. They say, just do your thing, and then you just sit there quietly. But I love the rehearsal hall. So I would love to just stay in the room regardless. So I'm staying in the room because I would rather be there than outside in the greenroom. I would stay in there because maybe I'm dance captain now, so I have to be there, or stay there because I'm in the ensemble and I'm understudying somebody. For whatever those reasons were.

So then you get to be a student of the room of not just the actors, but of the whole room. You get to watch stage managers chat with choreographers, you get to watch choreographers chat with directors. You get to watch designers come in. You get to watch everybody come in and communicate and you can see where things are going right and you can see where people are missing things. I started having conversations with myself about what I was seeing. About the art that was being made and the process around it. All these other moving parts. And at first I'd say, oh, I'm just making up a story. But I'd literally be like, oh, you're saying this and oh, you didn't tell her the right way because I see what she did there. And it was this great game that I had and that I was creating. And then I realized it wasn't a story. I was reading the room. Okay, well, this is fun. And it was dynamic, the idea of what is the container or the space in which you create the art? What are the ways of communicating which create the best art? What are the conversations or the silences to allow that other person that needs to be heard to get them on board? And all of those things I became incredibly interested in. And I said, I wonder if I might be a director. I started having those conversations over several shows. And it came to a point where, I would almost bubble over and offer something which would absolutely not be my place. So, once I had to choke it down for two good shows in a row, I thought, this might be something. Let's go see if I'm more than talented, if I have an aptitude for it. Just like with anything, talent is one thing, but I thought there had to be a certain aptitude for it. And I was like, I don't know if I have that. So let's go find out.

**I love what you offered as a student of the room. What a way of perfectly summarizing, as a practitioner, all of the things that you'd need to have and do in order to actually be sensitive to doing this work properly.**

It's a beautiful thing, too. Because you almost feel like you're in the eye of the storm in that way. Everything is swirling around you and you have to then focus on which story I'm going to pay attention to right now. Because there's so much happening in this room. And that's when I remember, I kept on following most of the conversations between the director and somebody. And I was like, I think this is the story that I'm interested in right here. It's beautiful. It's beautiful to be a student of the room, especially if it doesn't feel oppressive.

**Because we are in such a movement-based form, was there ever a moment where you thought you should do both choreography and directing? I know you continue to still do both in different ways. But when they came together, what was that like?**

I think they don't exist apart for me. It's just about the language that the piece of art demands me to use. As long as there are bodies in space, then it must be dance for me. They cannot not be dancing if bodies are there. Whether it's something that we can recognize or not, a moving body in space is dancing. They're telling us a story. There is a language of the body that must be there because there are humans there. It just depends. And the music for me: because I come to theatre through dance, there's always music. That's the way that I treat my plays. Plays are word music. It's a word composition, but it is music to me. Doing something like *Man and Superman*, which is six hours long, and people asked, well, how do you do it? It's amazing because that to me was an opera. It was the highest expression. Maybe we don't have the orchestra on stage with us, but this is an opera. This is six hours of word music by George Bernard Shaw. And I have all of these bodies, so they are naturally dancing now. And when we do scene work, especially for me, for Shaw I talk about the music and we break it down and I ask what's the time signature? That's how I do my scene work. What's the time signature? Great, and your punctuation then what? Is that a bar line? Is that a fermata? What are the dynamic markings in it? This is how I do my work. And then all of a sudden I'm like, oh, did you feel that? Oh, that time signature I was like we just went into a six eight. And then the counterpoint. That's the way that I break down text on top of everything else. Of course, there's intention and all these important things that are a part of it. But for me it is especially the music.

**It's such a beautiful luxury for me. One of my favourite reasons for being in a room with you is you show a willingness to meet others in the room at the language which they speak. I wish I could reciprocate more in some ways when it comes to movement and form on that level. It just warms my heart because, as a music director, I've always thought, I have to know what specific musical elements activate something dramaturgically in a very literal sense. And you do the same thing. And that symbiosis of it is that you have the score when you work.**

But you have to, because that's the whole reason that it's a musical, right? Because the score holds the rest of the keys and the secrets that our playwright or our librettist has in there. And then we go into songs, so then there are secrets in there. And the score has more secrets. You can't do it without; that's why it needed to be a musical. That's the other language that's happening. So you've got the script, and they don't exist as silos, but they're like sinus waves. And it depends where you are in the show, where in which arc of which character, everything's just oscillating like sinus waves. The script has one. And then the music has the other. For the choreographer, this is what's so amazing, because the choreographer has to write language that is not there. The musicians have notes. The actors have text.

So how do you create a language that works in line with these other two things, but also can naturally need to be its own count when it needs to be too, because you need to have that tension. That's what I think is so amazing about choreographers. They're just writing that language. But it needs to be informed by the text and it needs to be informed by the score. And it's all just beautiful. That's what's great about what we're finding out in this greater thing of what we are trying to do in art right now, is how multilingual you have to be. You have to invite multiple languages and at least want to learn about them in the space. And I'm using language as a big, big thing. It's about being multilingual and that the most creative spaces have to be multilingual.

**The best work happens when as many people as possible feel like they can speak their own language because everybody's understanding each other.**

And when you put them together under the baton of somebody brilliant, then here's your orchestra.

**I think part of what makes you such a rock star in the industry is that people are drawn to seeing artistic fluidity that holds true understanding and sensitivity to the different realms in which you're working. For you to be able to do Shaw effortlessly and then to move back into musical theatre, that's not easy.**

It's not, and I think the best part is that that's about my own hard work because it's my relationship to those pieces of work. I am the consistent thread through those things in the most selfish but thoughtful ways. It's my relationship to those things. Do I know them? Am I familiar? Am I invested? Am I studying? Am I enthralled with them? And also, am I critical with them? Because to love something is not to love something blindly. It's also to love it, and to be critical with it, and to identify shortcomings and to just say, this will be an obstacle. It's not necessarily my job, if I'm directing it, to solve everything, because it's been programmed. And to be really brave as an artist is to stand with it, and to shake it up and to let it stand in front of other people, and to not try and solve it. For me to fix it, I might get into a crazy place where I think, am I fixing it for a moral reason or am I fixing it for a structural reason? Because, either way, I don't know if I necessarily want to do that. And these are the big moral questions right now. But I think in terms of moving back and forth between different, high forms of art is about making sure that I'm studying them, that I respect them, and that I have a relationship with them. So I'm still a student of them.

**One of the things I love seeing is the sensitivity you bring to being in an audition room. Something as simple as coming out from outside around the table, which seems so simple. Do you have a philosophy that sort of drives each audition room you come into and does it shift often?**

In my head, I know that it doesn't feel like it, but I wish that it felt like the actors were auditioning me as equally as I'm auditioning them. If there was not a scarcity of work and actors could choose us, I would have to be the kind of director and demonstrate it in the audition that would show myself and the room that I would hope to have them in. So it's about me auditioning for every single person.

**Amen to that.**

It's about breaking some of those rules. So, coming out to greet people. If I have time, I will go get you because I want you to know that I would stand up and open the door for you. That I don't need to sit in this pretend throne behind this pretend desk. I will absolutely come and open the door for you. You know why? Because, on top of everything else, you're not getting paid for today. You have invested in this, you have taken your lessons. And I mean, not just the lesson or the coaching before but lessons for years. You've gotten on the subway or the bus. You travelled in, packed your bag, ironed your clothes, you've gone through the music. This has been a culmination of so much. So, I can go open the door. I can stand up and go around the table and say hello. I can ask you and give you the opportunity to do something twice. Absolutely.

If you were not cast when you leave this room, my legacy needs to be that you felt respected and seen and that you were given the opportunity to do the best job that you could in that moment. That is my responsibility. Being a leader in the room. And if we can't give them that, then we need to get out. I remember the first time I was in New York for *Hairspray* to go run one of the open calls. And I remember I couldn't sleep that night I was so excited. I couldn't believe it. I am in New York to go run an open call for this. I was like, I hope no one knows that it's just me, Kimmy Rampersad. I was so excited that I jumped out of the hotel room, put my New York scarf around my neck. Got my mocha latte, skipping down to Kelsey Studios. I pivot, turn, kick ball change into there. And I go up there and we're running these auditions. The casting director is there and the young people are coming in and, for *Hairspray*, first we audition the young people for the ensemble in two big groups: the Motormouth kids and the Nicest Kids. The Nicest Kids would come in and the casting director says, "Hey, this is Kimmy Rampersad. She's the associate choreographer on the tour and she's going to be leading you in your auditions today." And the kids would smile, and it would be great. And then it was the first time that a group of Motormouth kids came in. The casting director said, "Hi, this is Kimmy Rampersad, and she's the associate choreographer." And I didn't know what was happening, but the look of my peers looking at me hit me. I didn't know at first what was happening. I said, Okay, I'm gonna lead you. This was many years ago, but I was starting the practice of trying to make sure everyone felt good.

There was this one sweet gentleman that left me a little note that just said, you made me feel really good about that process today. And I was like, that's what I want. I don't need people to write me notes but I really do want and need people in the best way to feel seen. And I think that, honestly, probably comes from a lot of my heartache that I'm trying to rectify in the universe of not being seen, not feeling seen, being dismissed, not whatever. And there needs to be a little more equality and room for people. The audition process is very important to me. All of those artists auditioning and going out; that's a bigger legacy than when you get to a company and work there.

**I'll never forget the simplest gestures like you leaving a note on my stand. And it was the first thing I saw at the start of every single show. And I still have it, and it went with me home to New York. It let me know that I was seen in that moment and every moment after.**

That's important to me. I hope that I always can build in more capacity to see everyone and to let them know. That's how we build great people to make great art.

**With _The Color Purple_, one of the most startling things for me was trying to find not only another woman who had directed it, but another woman of color.**

I remember when I saw that article [describing her being the first woman of color to direct the show], I was like, are you serious? Who's been directing this? I mean, I hope that I don't have to be Irish if I wanted to direct something like _Dancing at Lughnasa_ but, we're talking about shows that are so close to hurt and trauma, and we're talking about shows from communities that are still underrepresented, misrepresented, where there are not enough of those people in those communities in positions of leadership and ownership and agency and voice. It does really speak to the system in which we operate. It's more of an indictment than some sort of illumination. I don't know who keeps track of stats like that but if I am the first Black and Brown girl to direct *The Color Purple* professionally, then that's what that is. And that is quite an honor. But that is also something for our industry and our community to think, why is that? Are we proud of that? Are we okay with that? And if we're not, what are our practices to address that? It's such a mixed kind of thing.

**It stings as much as it's beautiful because we have to cross that mark.**

Exactly, and that took a lot of work. And although I'm the person who's the recipient of that acknowledgement, it is not about me; it's about everybody that came before me to position me for this moment right here. So that's why I could never poo poo it because it isn't about me. It's about how I was positioned through everybody's work in the industry, from my family, and through ancestors of people that are mine and distantly of mine, we're all connected. It's like a wave that came up and I just happened to be the person who might be at the front of this little pyramid for a second. But that crown has been made and forged by many people before and I just get to take it for a second. And now it's off of my head and in the right way, it's going to pass on to somebody else.

**It's a life changing show (The Color Purple), right? I never could have prepared for what that had in store for all of us.**

Never. I could have never known. Which is kind of good because I think if I knew how big and how much the cost, the joy of it, and why it cost so much, I wonder if I would have done it. I mean, I would have done it. I couldn't even fathom if someone even told me what it would be. I don't think I could fathom what we all created together.

**So important for it to be seen across the country in Canada. I remember getting out West to see it, and that moment of sitting in the audience and seeing us on stage. That's what this is, this moment, right here. Just the collective understanding of what we were trying to bring to that whole story and its existence in many forms and through many bodies. To try and convey that must have been really, really special.**

It was because you just think about how many Black communities there are across any space, but especially in Canada. You think about, especially in Alberta, these are her people that ended up immigrating north through Oklahoma as people came up to Red Valley. This is the story of their people before they made this move. When we were in Winnipeg, you still think about those people that came up centrally, and also the porters and everybody that came through the railroad from Nova Scotia where we were putting the show on. You see this great intersection again, in the heart of our continent, of this story that comes from a particular community. That speaks to greater communities because of the humanity. It was beautiful. It was really important.

**When we talk about mentorship in the industry, and particularly in these conversations, has there been a mentor who's been directly in line with you or somebody who hasn't? How has that resonated with you and why?**

Mentorship for me is important. It's a part of my artistic practice. It's a part of me being an artist, it's a part of sharing if and when I learn things. It's important to be available to younger people, to support them, and important that I can be a safe place where they can bounce ideas off of, that I can be loving and critical if they want it, or sometimes if they don't, but if I hopefully, thoughtfully invested that I can offer something or a different point of view. So those things are important. I think that's a part of traditions that are not just written; those are oral traditions and different ways that we share and pass knowledge. And, again, because we are in this great tradition of storytelling, I think that mentorship plays such a part and it's such a natural part of artistic practice for me. So mentorship is incredibly important. Of the mentors that I've had, and I've had a few, the most significant would be Philip Akin. He taught me the importance of mentorship and I've inherited that from him. So that's a part of my artistic inheritance from him. And I'm very happy and proud to even be associated with him. And I think what's amazing is that he has so many people that would say the same thing about him.

**Absolutely. He was a huge mentor for me too; for so many Black artists in Canada.**

So, in the best way, I'm not special. Because he shows this kindness to everyone. I'm not special, but he is special to me. That is wonderful. So he's been very important to me. In terms of like influences from other people: Sammy Davis Jr. Absolutely influential. Jessye Norman. Absolutely influential. You know who else has been influential? Pierre Elliot Trudeau. As a leader. Those are some people. I know, very different.

**Especially for us in theatre, it's important to consider the outside too. We don't exist in a bubble.**

It's so interesting. You know, I picked political science because I was interested in it. I just didn't want to do it for my life. But I certainly have a passion for it. I love it. I love reading about it. I love doing those things. I just didn't want to do it. But it's so amazing now to find out where I am. And to see how everything is just crashing together. It's all just coming together. It's just crazy and awesome but I think that's important as artists though. Anything that we do, our study makes our art better. It's all an investment in us and our lens and what we can speak to and the places and the things that we can make connections to. Art is about making connections. The better and the bolder that we live the well curated life is a life that we can make more meaning and connections with our art. Which is beautiful. Like tentacles going out. It's a very hard thing to learn early on.

**You're the Associate Artistic Director at the Shaw Festival in Niagara-on-the-Lake, Canada, which is massive on all North American standards for theatre. What do you hope for? What do you look forward to in the future with your post?**

I think, especially here at the Shaw, I am interested in developing, programming, and populating the season with plays from Shaw and his contemporaries from the world. Not just contemporaries that look like him; not just contemporaries that speak the same first language. That when we say Shaw and his contemporaries, that there are incredible playwrights from across the face of this globe who have written extraordinary work. Just like the same idea when people use the term classic, which is a very loaded, non-specific term: classic and classical. But when we use those things, that idea of if that's a time period, is that a sensibility? Is that a style? However we're defining it, it doesn't happen in isolation and there's a whole world that happens with it. I'm interested in that.

I'm interested in all of our spaces being populated with the best and the brightest, and that we learn that best and bright is not one thing. It presents itself in a myriad of ways. In ways that we don't even know. And how do we become open to that? When we're challenged with not recognizing it, how do we not close the door but open ourselves to surrender and realize that, especially as leaders, surrender doesn't mean that you have to surrender leadership. I think I'm interested in spaces where leadership is about who is always willing to pass the ball first. I think that's who the leader is. I've got the ball. I see you need the ball. I'm passing it to you. I've got the ball. I see who needs it next. You pass it to people who don't even think they want the ball, but you realize they should have the ball right now. And the trust that you build in the space so people will keep passing you the ball if they don't know what to do because they'll trust you to pass the ball to the best person. Leadership isn't about holding on to it. It's about knowing where that agency needs to go. And you will receive the ball more only because you're going to be the one who's passing it well. But then, guess what happens: people will learn how to pass it well with you. And now it's just a roomful of leaders passing the ball.

**What would you say to the young artists entering, looking at you saying, if she can do this I can do this?**

Damn right. Damn skippy. And better and more elegantly and deeper. You will be and you must necessarily be. We will all help you do that. But absolutely, if I can do it, you could do it with your own stank, your own bravado, your own shoulder. In your own way on your own time. In your own way. I can't say that enough. People always like to say, well, this is their path, their trajectory. Everybody's path is different. So different.

# RICK SORDELET

 **Rick Sordelet** is the United States'
premier Fight Director. He has seventy-
two Broadway shows to his credit. He
has staged many of Disney Theatricals'
productions, including *The Lion King*,
*Beauty and the Beast*, *Tarzan*, *Aida*, and
*The Little Mermaid*, as well as hundreds
of productions Off-Broadway and in regional theatre.

He is also the only Fight Director to ever stage the fights for a
Superbowl Halftime Show at Superbowl XXIX.

Rick teaches at Yale School of Drama and HB Studio in NYC.
He has also taught at the Neighborhood Playhouse, NYU, and
the New School of Drama in New York City, and sits on the
board for the Shakespeare Theatre of New Jersey.

Rick has staged stunts and fights for over a thousand
episodes of *Guiding Light* during his twelve years as their Chief
Stunt Coordinator.

He and David Blix are partners in Sordelet Inc, an electronic
publishing house. www.sordeletinc.com.

**What was the first moment of getting into theatre? How did musical theatre get introduced to you?**

I got hurt playing sports in high school. And there was a young lady who was in the musical theatre programme at our high school. When I say programme, believe me . . . It was Hermantown, Minnesota. There wasn't a programme. Miss Gryphon, who was twenty-four years old and fresh out of college, was the really enthusiastic, lovely person who was leading it. They were doing *Once Upon a Mattress*, so I auditioned for King Sextimus. I didn't have to sing, I didn't have any lines, I just had to pantomime and it was a gas. I had so much fun. So then I started doing the plays and other musicals there and I decided that I wanted to be a performer.

So, this is is unreal: I didn't take the SATs. I took no pre-college anything. I walked into the Registrar's Office at the University of Wisconsin-Superior. I said, "I want to go to school here." And they said, okay. So one of the guys, John Wojohowitz, we called him Wojo; he got in touch with one of the people that would be one of those mentors of your life. His name was John Mencell. He called John and I imagine the conversation was like, "Oh my god, we got this rube from Hermantown, Minnesota, here with a chequebook ready to go to college", and John must have said, "Alright, what do we need to do?" So, they got my transcripts, and they paved the way. I have no idea how it happened. All I know is that I wrote a check for $283 and I was in college.

I walked into a class that this guy Bill Stock was teaching, and sitting there was my lifelong friend Brenda Hutaree, who had been a Chisholm Minnesota cheerleader. Earlier that year, I saw her and her Chisholm cheerleaders at the McDonald's where we all hung out. I was giving her a whole bunch of crap about how I was gonna go to the Children's Theatre and be an actor, and she said, oh, I'm going to UWS. I'm like, please, who goes there. But, after a good time of rubbing my nose in it, we just became solid friends. You make those kinds of friends where you bond and you become so close. None of us knew what we were doing. None of us. We just knew nothing. And so we were in this really great programme, at a small university. And they would toss you the keys and they would say, go make theatre. If you break it, tell us; if you spill it, clean it up and make sure you turn off the lights when you leave. And it was the greatest four years I ever spent in theatre, which was awesome.

From there, I started doing stage combat with another one of my mentors, Albert Katz. Albert was the only American at that time to have written a book on stage combat. He was one of the founders of the Society of American Fight Directors. So he was a big stage combat superstar in that tiny little world. And so, my freshman year, I walked into his office, and I said, "Hey, I should apprentice with you." And he said, you should get out of my office. But I convinced him that this would be a good deal. I took the class as a freshman, and you were only supposed to take the class as a senior. I took the class every time he offered it, and so, by my junior year, he said you're going to teach the class, and I'm going to watch you teach. And then every Tuesday and Thursday, I would have to go into his office and I would have to defend how I was teaching. So, he taught me a great deal about how to teach. He's a master teacher. He was excellent.

Then the next year, my senior year, I taught the class on my own. And I was also teaching at the school across the bay in Duluth at University of Minnesota-Duluth. And so they said, look, you got a talent. We should try and get you into grad school and this could pay your way. The URTAs, which is the University Resident Theatre Association, were happening. So, my friend Mike Hill and I hitchhiked and took buses down to Evanston, Illinois. We wrote to people to meet with them in their hotel. And was gonna go to Cornell. That was the school that offered me the most money. It was a free ride. I was going to teach, get an MFA. All great. So I'm on the elevator, and another lifelong friend who I'm currently working for at Kean University, Holly Rhodes, was on the elevator. So, I was kind of bragging to her. And the guy in the back of the elevator thinks it's hilarious. And it's William Esper. So, he says, would you like to audition for Rutgers? I say, "sure, why not, I don't care." Holly says, do you know who that is? You know where Rutgers is? I don't know anything. So I went to his hotel room. We audition. He likes my work. He says, look, I'm interested in you as an actor. I don't really care about you as a fight director. I don't care if you teach at my school or not. We'll have you do it but I'm interested in you becoming an actor. And I say, so how much are you going to pay me? And he says nothing. Nothing the first semester. I don't even know if I'm going to keep you or not. Little did I know at that time that, in the programme that Bill was running at Rutgers, we started with twenty-three students and ended with eleven. I mean, they just kicked people out. Something they don't do now. Or, if you do, you have to be very careful about kicking out a student now, you'd have to really have academic proof. For Bill, it was easy as, you talked back to me, and I don't think you're going to be a good fit, so get out.

**Times have changed!**

So, I called my mom that night and I told her about everything. I told her about all the different schools that were interested in me. And then I told her about this Bill Esper guy and said that he was interested in me as an actor and didn't care about stage combat. I thought she was going to say, what a jerk this guy is. And she was kind of quiet. She said, he's the only one who talked to you about being an actor. You really should really consider. Once, I looked him up, I realized that he was one of the foremost acting teachers in the country. So I went to Rutgers. And, while at Rutgers, true to his word, I didn't teach the first semester. I had to win him over. I stayed and I became a peer teacher. So I was on faculty, but also teaching my peers. And then I stayed at Rutgers. I graduated in 1985. I was there till 1987 teaching. And then I went out, and started being an actor/stage combatant. I would do Tybalt and stage the fights, or I would do Laertes and stage the fights. Then Rob Roth, the director of *Beauty and the Beast*, called me up and said, I'd like you to do *Beauty and the Beast* on Broadway. And I hung up the phone, looked at my wife, and I said, that's it, I'm going to become a full time fight director. And that's all I'm going to do. And that was the day that I just went, that's it. I made a vow that I would treat fight directing the same way that I treated acting: as a craft. And I would put my full attention into how the craft of stage combat works. And so embracing the term, behaving truthfully under imaginary circumstances, is how I built my career. And then from *Beauty and the Beast*, coincidentally, *Once Upon a Mattress* was my second show, and then *Titanic, Jekyll and Hyde, Lion King*. And by then I was just kicking in. I did the halftime show at Super Bowl XXIX. I'm the only fight director to have ever done the Super Bowl.

**That's amazing!**

Once things started cooking, I started going around the world and doing all these shows. We did *The Lion King* and *Beauty and the Beast* everywhere. We did thirty-four first class productions of *Beauty and the Beast* and about the same, maybe more, for *The Lion King*. I was there at the very beginning when Disney Theatricals started.

**How did you know fight direction was what you wanted to do?**

There was something about working with a director. I imagine it's a lot like when you're conducting. I remember Paul Gemigniani said, I am an actor that the actors work with, but I'm not on stage. When I deliver the music, I'm delivering the music as another actor. It's great knowing that the work you're doing is making that show fly. Similarly, I liked when I worked with the director. If you were directing *Romeo and Juliet* and someone said, "I have this idea". That's the most exciting thing I can hear from a director. Then you start laying out your vision, you start talking about this is what I'd like to see happen. This is what I want the audience to feel. If the director could stage their own fights, they would. Just like if the director could conduct their own music, they would. But they have to go to the spokes of the hub.

**The true collaboration in theatre.**

So, if the directors are the hub, then we are a necessary part of the wheel that helps to make it turn. So, the director will talk to you about what they want. They'll talk to me about what they want, and then we'll put our values together to create a collaborative story that I hope doesn't have the script line that says, oh, here's the fight scene. I like when it just unfolds organically and, all of a sudden, you're just fighting because you have nothing else you can do. And you see this all the time in music, when a character is so filled with emotion and the only thing next that they can do is sing. That's beautiful. That's one of the things that I love about Tevye. "If I Were a Rich Man" just comes boiling out of him. "Tradition" just comes boiling out of him. It's what happens when we see our greatest numbers. They come out of a place where there's nothing else but that appropriate thing to do. The trick for me is using the last line before the fight and the first line after the fight. What happened that made me say the first line after the fight? Same is true of the song. What happens before the song starts? What happens after the song ends? What did we learn and what has moved?

When we did *Scarlet Pimpernel*, there was no reason for the fight. I said to the composer Frank Wildhorn, the writer Nan Knighton, and the director Peter Hunt, why are we fighting? Because, right now, nothing happens to provoke it and I explain all the reasons why. Peter looks at me and goes, "Because it's fucking cool. I'm looking for the eleventh-hour fight, and I just want people to fight. It's just something the audience needs." Frank said, "I wrote this really cool music which we didn't use." So, in terms of that, sometimes approaching the work like that gets you in trouble. Sometimes the director gets scared of having another director in the room. They get afraid. I just literally had this happen this week, where the director said, I feel like I can't work with you on

*Three Musketeers* because you directed it and I haven't. What does that have to do with anything? I did *Romeo and Juliet* and I had a director who was younger, and she said, oh my God, I feel like I'm working with my Dad. And I said, well, that's on you. I'm not your Dad. I'm your collaborator. But, if that's what you're bringing to the table, how do you want to proceed?

**You're describing musical theatre perfectly: the truest form of not collaboration. To go from singing to fighting in a musical: they're both vehicles for expressing action and what is happening, but to have those two worlds coexist so closely to one another is a fascinating thing. Have you stuck largely to being a fight director or do you choreograph as well?**

It's interesting. As a fight director, when I come in the director says, I'm doing *Romeo and Juliet* and I want to do this. Then you get up and say, I want Tybalt and Romeo to go here, then up the stairs, and then down these other stairs and fight over here. This is where I want Tybalt to stab Mercutio and this is where I want Tybalt to be killed. Great. Now I'll choreograph what you have directed so I become a fight choreographer. When I work for someone and they say, from Act Three, Scene One, when the bell rings, I want this to happen. I want the audience to feel this. And I want to go right up until "Fortune's Fool". So, for that section, I'm fight directing based on the notes of the director, but directing the scene. Part of my job is to make sure that I can create a seamless connection to the arc of your storytelling as a director, and that no one would be able to discern that this is my style and this is yours. This is your story. Which is why I was so saddened when this director bypassed an opportunity for us to collaborate because they clearly let their own ego get in the way of their own insecurities, and didn't embrace the fact that as a fight director, I'm not interested in directing this. I'm only interested in telling your story.

**That's very cool. I've never really heard fight choreographer and fight director delineated in such specific individual terms. They both lend themselves to different ways of collaborating with the rest of the team which is really interesting.**

One of the things that I was deeply impressed that you're doing is now you're talking about this from another lens. I'm almost ashamed to say that I've skated along on a complete white privilege in the past. I learned this lesson when I went into the Super Bowl meeting. My wife took me to The Gap. And she said, if you're going to go down there, you're going to need to look like them. And we bought khakis, and those kinds of shirts. I went down there and I didn't even look like what I usually look like. Normally, I'm just a T-shirt and jeans guy. If I want to dress up, I'll put a button-down with my jeans. But I went in there and I looked like the executives. And I think there was a comfort in that as there would be in any culture that you go into where, if the people who are the movers and shakers of the culture look at you and see that you understand their culture, there's going to be an affinity to that.

I looked at some of the people who were there like the stunt coordinators. There was one guy who came in with a leather vest and he had a goatee and a ponytail and leather cap and he didn't fit. It wasn't that he was any better or anything else. I just happened to understand the corporate culture enough to take that. That was based on growing up in high school in Northern Minnesota, where it was not uncommon for someone to wear a T-shirt that said, "Save a Coho, Kill An Indian." And that was because Natives had fishing rights year round and that angered the fisherman. People just assumed that I was white. They assumed that I felt like they did. And nobody cared until the last ten years to even ask you what you identified as. I took the advice of my grandmother, and I just stayed quiet. She'd say, "you tell anybody you're Indian, you're gonna get knocked down. So enjoy that. Don't make a thing out of it." It wasn't until I was in my thirties that I finally was like, no, I'm Native and I don't give a fuck. This is who I am. This is part of what I grew up with. My mom was a housing director on the Fond du Lac Reservation. She has a building named after her, and she put people in houses that never even lived in a house before.

**That's quite the legacy to not have shared for so late into your career. I'm curious as far as the industry and your work in musical theatre. Did you have no opportunity to share or interact with that part of your identity?**

During that time that I was coming up, when I did share it, everybody was like, oh, that's cool. Whatever. Nobody cared. Could you do the job? That's what mattered. There's a difference. I'm glad to see the word BIPOC being used. For a while when people talk about people of color, they've exclusively meant Black. And that's what I meant too when I talked about people of color. When we talked about inclusion and equality, nobody was really talking about Natives or Asians, they were talking about Black people in particular. And I don't give a fuck; if that's the first step, then let that be the first step. And it has been a great first step and there's been so much progress.

You know, this is very controversial, but the thing that does anger me is when I do see a lot of people of color start to slap at the allies that are still holding their hands out. Especially in the theatre culture. I once said, it's easy to smack at the low hanging fruit of white people in theatre. I'm going to be more impressed when you're in the boardrooms of Goldman Sachs and on Wall Street. I'm really looking forward to the day that your company goes in there and does for them what you've done for theatre. Because at the end of the day, they're the ones controlling the purse strings. So we can sit here and we can buzzsaw our way through all this stuff. But I've been a board president for two years. I know how little money is out there from corporations for not for profit. I know how much not for profit is actually hated by a lot of the presidents of big corporations because their feeling is that you all make us as conservatives look like the villains, so I'd rather give my money elsewhere than to a theatre that's going to programme corporate America as the villain. So we're all left scrambling. You're out there trying to get money to help each other; meanwhile, there's this infighting going on. Instead, join forces and let's figure this out together, and mostly, let's tell our stories so the rest of America can catch up and actually do something about it.

**Has there ever been a point where some sort of Native narrative has been a part of a musical that you've been a part of?**

Once. It was one of the last plays I did at Yale Rep. It's called *Mannahatta*. The author was writing a dual story between now and what it was like for the Manhattan Indians to give up the land to the Dutch. It was one of those things where, my entire life, I have never been lauded for being Native, until I walked in the room. And it was like, oh, finally, a Native fight director, oh, my God! But it didn't make me feel good. It made me feel like, suddenly, we were having this big conversation about me being Native and that somehow that was going to make the fight directing better. That's so off the mark in my opinion. Me being Native did nothing more than me being Native. That's it. But me being a fight director and helping tell the story was really why I was there. But then, there was this moment of, "oh, aren't we all really groovy that we're all Natives doing this?" It's like, yeah, but we're still a small culture in a bigger culture, in a bigger culture telling a story about this culture. I didn't want to lose sight of that. Nor did I feel comfortable really grooving into that. Part of that was my own feelings of, am I Native enough? Or will they say, oh, well, now, you're going to claim your Nativeness now that you're here. Where was all your Nativeness on *The Lion King*?

**This is why I'm so excited to speak to you: look at the depth to which we can explore being a person of color in this industry.**

**There's many layers. Not only do we have to meet the rainbow of identity that exists, but we have to also acknowledge at some point that we are doing this about the work and we're doing this about being in rooms where we need to tell human stories. Do we need to feature more stories of people who are going to be in that rainbow? Of course we do. We really do. But the basis of all this is that we should have all been doing everything anyways. You can't just be called to be a fight director in a room on only Native productions. Because if that were the case, well, where would we even be?**

You really hit the nail on the head beautifully. I like to identify as a storyteller in our business. My luckiness was so amazing. Right off the bat at Rutgers, I got in with Ricardo Khan and Lee Richardson. I became their resident fight director at Crossroads. I'm this young guy who looks white, and I'm doing one play after another with Black performers. And no problem. Never once did anyone have a problem. And Marshall Jones, he's one of my greatest friends. I think that I could attribute so much of my comfort going into identifying and embracing everything of who I am to the countless hours of talking with Marshall. And, I mean, countless hours. He is one of the most beautiful human beings. And what I love about Marshall is he's currently directing a play about Oscar Wilde. He advocated that him being a Black director is inconsequential to the storytelling. You don't need an Englishman to come over and tell the story about Oscar Wilde any more than you need a French person to tell the story of *The Three Musketeers*. If you have a storyteller who can tell the story, then tell the story. And the producers were like, right on. And to me, Marshall epitomizes where I want to see our industry go. Liesl Tommy is one of the best directors I've ever worked with. I love working with Liesl

Tommy, but Liesl Tommy should not be relegated to just doing stories about Black people.

**Of course not!**

She's going to know how to get to the heart of the matter from a humanitarian point of view. She's a humanitarian. So you say, that's where I want to see this. And there should be an entire all-Black creative team doing *The Music Man* with an all-white cast. Now, the double-edged sword is the second I say I want to direct August Wilson, we're going to bump into problems. But I'm going to honor August Wilson, because he said, my work should only be directed by Black directors. And he is absolutely right. One hundred percent. Because I'm never going to bring to the table culturally what Marshall Jones would be able to do. But Marshall would be able to bring to the table everything I can bring to *The Three Musketeers*. So, as an artist, there are some areas where you just respect it. Edward Albee says there's certain things that he'll never let happen with *Who's Afraid of Virginia Woolf?* Because he doesn't want to fuck with it.

We had a director from Yale, and she wanted to set it in a worldwide wrestling ring. And they [the estate] said, very politely, no. That's not going to happen. So, you just end up respecting what the artist wants, like you would with August. You just go, great. I don't see any reason why you would need to bend that to prove some kind of a point. Could Dan Sullivan direct August Wilson? Absolutely. Would kill it. But Dan Sullivan would be missing one important step. So is there a world where we all can do that? Absolutely. One hundred percent. Could we make it happen? Yes. And why? Because there's going to be people who understand it, and are willing to talk about it because that's the other thing. Everybody's so scared of each other. They're afraid to say anything. And then worried about proving how woke they are or proving to this other person that happens to be Black or BIPOC, I get it. So that's where I see the value of people that get it, like you. Especially as a young man going into this business. You're the change I'm looking for. I had my shot in a way. I danced in my light. It's not out but I'm on the fringe. You're the future.

**We can't be afraid of that. We can't be afraid of each other either. That's why we come to this art of all things. Any one of us could have been an accountant or a banker. There's a reason we're not. We believe**

in the theatre to be a nurturer and healer of the human condition. And, if we're going to get into a point of being afraid of it or afraid of each other in the stories we can tell through it, then that's just terrifying.

It sometimes feels to me like the pendulum is never going to come to center. I feel like, during the pandemic in particular, we felt it swing. And we just sort of pulled the curtain aside and it freaked everybody out. Suddenly, these theatres were hiring artistic associates. The color scheme changed on the staff page. But I'm willing to take that step. If that's the step and it wants to be performative, good. Because from that performative step comes real steps.

Exactly, because at some point, everything gets thrown into the air, and it's all floating. Then at some point, everything settles. We've had extensive conversations about this in the industry. You may get endless calls like, hey, who's the woman of color that I can call and put on a stand to do this. It's not that people have been standing at the door not able to get through. We haven't set the sign out saying line up here. This is what we're talking about when we talk about structural work. Now you want to get all of these people in here, but you haven't enabled people from those communities to access these stories. You haven't provided the resource for them to be able to have the same training, the same exposure, the same networking opportunities that we all know you need in order to succeed in this business. You got to go way back. It's going to be uncomfortable. It's going to take time.

Do you remember the Wells Fargo president who really stepped in it when he asked where all the people of color were? And he said, they're not here. He messed up because what he should have said is, we see the need to create opportunity and so we are now going to be opening up all these programmes to start developing young people who can take these jobs. Which is exactly why Sordelet Inc. decided to go back to the reservation. Just as you just pointed out, nobody's put the sign up, and so, Sordelet Inc. has now put the sign out. We want Indigenous people to start to explore the theatre through our assets and then see what they like and see if this is something they can do. If the reservation can help them and there's opportunity, then that's what we should be doing. And, ten years from now, I am so looking forward to seeing a bright rainbow of fight directors filled with all kinds of different people so that nobody gets a phone call from some white producers shopping for their ethnicity. Just looking for the day when someone says, this person is really good at this. Let's hire them. That's what we're going for. And I just so respect what you're doing. I think what you're doing is so needed. Thank you for just stepping in.

**If just if one student gets this book in their hands, and they say, I'm doing this art as a result of reading this and reading about Rick feeling like he passed as white like me, and I have a place in this industry too, then we're golden.**

The sad truth is on the other side of the coin: I'm still looked at as an old white man. And, man, it is brutal. Yeah. I think, if anything, the thing that shames our community is the hypocrisy. Ageism. The way that they we treat older people. The way that we treat white people right now is just shocking.

**We have to be careful. We have to remember why we do this too. There's no exclusivity in theatre. We have to believe we can all come to the table equally. We have to.**

You said it earlier, we could have all been accountants. If I put this much energy into just getting rich I'd have been on Wall Street taking people's money. You and I wake up the same way. We wake up feeling very lucky that we go into the theatre. And I imagine when you pick up the baton, it's the same thing I feel when I pick up a sword. I feel so grateful to be telling stories. Our brotherhood lies there. When I look at you, I see a man who is me. You're a story. I'm a story. Both of us coming from different cultural experiences. I can recognize how hard it was for you. I can recognize that for you, you had to be twenty times more than everybody else because you wouldn't be one of the few in it now if you weren't.

**Never has there been a stronger truth, and we know that because we've lived it our whole lives.**

For me, it was looking back at the reservation and knowing what I didn't want to go back to. It was knowing that once you're out, you can go back, but you don't get out again as easy. When people talk about reservations I just say, Google Pine Ridge. Though I'm not Lakota, Pine Ridge is a national embarrassment. No people should live like that. No one. But it's allowed. And it's allowed because it's an easy door to keep closed. Someone's gotta kick it open and that's you, my friend. So, let's go to work.

**It's all of us. Rick, I can't thank you enough. Thank you so much for your time.**

# MASI ASARE

**Masi Asare** is a composer/lyricist, dramatist, and performance scholar. A Tony-nominated songwriter, her shows include *Paradise Square* (Broadway) and *Monsoon Wedding* (St. Ann's Warehouse, Doha/Qatar Creates). As a composer/lyricist/bookwriter, she has been commissioned by Theatre Royal Stratford East, the Lilly Awards, Barbara Whitman Productions/Grove Entertainment, and the Toulmin Foundation. Her shows in development include *The Family Resemblance* (book/music/lyrics), developed at the O'Neill Center and Live & In Color; *Rishvor* (book/music/lyrics), *Garden of Starflowers* (book/music/lyrics), and *Delta Blue* (music/lyrics). Masi's secret agent musical *Sympathy Jones* (music/lyrics/concept), and Marvel superhero play *Mirror of Most Value* have collectively had over 110 productions. A past Dramatists Guild Fellow, Masi won the inaugural Billie Burke Ziegfeld Award for a woman composer of musicals and has been honored with the Holof Lyricist Award and Haupt Composition Prize from the Eugene O'Neill Theatre Center, and an Emerging Artist Grant from the Theatre Hall of Fame. In 2021 she was named a "Woman to Watch on Broadway" by Broadway Women's Fund.

Masi's voice students have performed on Broadway and around the globe, and her scholarly book *Voicing the Possible: Technique, Vocal Sound, and Black Women on the Musical Stage* is forthcoming. Previously a Kaplan Institute for the

Humanities Faculty Fellow, she is presently co-editing a special issue of the academic journal *Studies in Musical Theatre* on "The Musical-Theatrical Global South," part of a research project supported by Northwestern's Buffett Institute for Global Affairs. She has presented at conferences for BroadwayCon; EMP PopCon; Song, Stage, and Screen (SSS); the American Musicological Society (AMS); the American Society for Theatre Research (ASTR); the Association for Theatre in Higher Education (ATHE); the Educational Theatre Association (EdTA); and the International Thespian Society (ITS). She has published with Samuel French/Concord Theatricals, the Rodgers and Hammerstein Organization, *Journal of Popular Music Studies*, *TDR*, *The Routledge Companion to Musical Theatre*, *Studies in Musical Theatre*, and *Performance Matters*.

Masi is on the faculty of the Theatre and Performance Studies departments at Northwestern University, where she teaches courses in musical theatre history, musical theatre writing, and vocal performance studies. In 2022 she received the Clarence Simon Award for Teaching and Mentoring from Northwestern's School of Communication. She is a member of ASCAP and the Dramatists Guild, a member of the editorial board of *Studies in Musical Theatre*, and an advisory board member for Maestra. Masi holds a bachelor's degree from Harvard and an MA and PhD from New York University's Tisch School of the Arts. She divides her time between Chicago and New York City. https://masiasare.com | @masiasare

**Was musical theatre always it for you?**

I loved musicals from the time I was very young. I don't come from a theatre family so they were like, what is this? This is a little embarrassing, but my family was very into the simple life and so we didn't have a television, so I didn't grow up watching movie musicals. But we were at a friend's home and I saw *The Sound of Music*. I think I was eleven years old and that was it for me. I was like, okay, well, this is it. You can have stories and music? What else is there? So from that point on, I was pretty obsessed. I had always taken piano lessons and was in the bands and orchestras in school, and when I was fourteen, I called the local theatre in my town. I grew up in a college town in Pennsylvania so the touring shows would come through. I called up and said, can I volunteer usher and I ushered for everything that came through town and I saw all kinds of things.

**I like that, because it's also such a great reminder that the theatre exists in so many forms and so many roles, and we're so thankful to all those people who help us execute that. From witnessing theatre regularly, what was the first move into doing it?**

Well, I did the high school productions, I did *Anything Goes*, I did a production at our local community theatre of *Bye Bye, Birdie*, I played in the orchestra. I was trombonist when I was growing up. I played in the orchestra for *Carnival*. I also played in the jazz band. I played piano, I played trombone, and I sang with the jazz band. We had a wonderful jazz band and we toured Europe. It was a great music program. I sang in the choirs. Then I got to college. The summer after my first year of college, I had a job outside of Boston at a children's theatre, and I was basically a camp counselor. But it was this wonderful program where they would write original musicals with the kids. And I continued working with that group into the fall and they asked me to put some new lyrics to existing songs. They said, take these songs and put some new lyrics that will fit our story. And I was like, I think I can write a song. So I just started writing songs for them. That was my college job. I wrote all these songs for these children's theatre productions. I always say that the kids were my first teachers because, if I wrote a melody that did not make sense, they would sing it in the way that made sense. They would just edit it. If there were too many words, I would find out real quick. I learned how to write songs that were singable. The stakes were very low. Parents were happy no matter what. And I learned how to underscore. I'd play the shows, and I'd underscore and I'd figure out, how do I bring this theme back to drive this dramatic moment? So that was my college job and that was my crash course.

**That's not a bad gig at all to have at that point. It sounds like it was really something that helped you figure out how you would access the art from multiple angles and viewpoints.**

Yeah. And for those shows, the idea was that we would write the shows with the kids. So they would do a lyric writing exercise and I would take all those pieces of paper home and use some of their rhymes and I would turn it around really quickly. The other thing that I really benefited from was that I learned to write fast. I was so young that I had no fear. I was like nineteen, twenty. I didn't have the anxiety that I wouldn't be good enough. I was just like, well, the kids need a song by tomorrow so I need to write a song. So I'm always really grateful for that sort of fearlessness.

**Where did you get the ability to write lyrics from?**

I always liked little word games and word puzzles. I always thought those were kind of fun. But I was thinking about this recently, I think it's because I sing a lot. So I know what feels good as a singer. I love to sing the work of great lyricists. I love to sing Sondheim. Sondheim sometimes terrifies me. I love him but then I feel depressed that I could never write something that good. I also love lyricists like Alan Jay Lerner who I think wrote such sharp, crisp, really singable lyrics. Lynn Ahrens. So I think the same way that you come up on a Kern melody or a Richard Rodgers melody and you just get this sense of, well, how can music lean into this dramatic moment? I think it was just spending time with these song books at the piano and I would sing through all these tunes. I think it was that exposure and that embodied practice of singing so that you know what feels good when you sing it; that vowel is not so great to sing high, that's too many consonants in a row, you know it as a singer in your body. So I think that has also been instilled as part of my practice.

**You went to Harvard and NYU?**

Yeah. I sometimes keep it quiet. Because when you say you went to Harvard, and then you do anything wrong, everyone's like, oh, look at Harvard. But the thing that I found is that, I had some wonderful teachers there, but when I got out of that school, it had zero currency in the theatre world. It was always, did you go to Juilliard? Did you go to NYU? Didn't matter how smart you were or you thought you were. I'm grateful for the education, grateful for the opportunity that I had, but I don't have any illusions that that made it easy to have a career in the theatre necessarily.

**That's interesting. Did you find that your scholarly path helped supplement your skills as a lyricist?**

I think probably what was most helpful for me about Harvard was that I did not easily fit into the categories of different majors or different academic programs or areas of study. So I ended up making my own major. And I think that was one of the biggest gifts I got from it. Being an artist, you do always have to make up your own path and there is no magical way that you take these classes, and you're done. No: it was a process of invention, even at the level of creativity, even at the level of what I'm going to study. What my major was going to be. I started as a music and English major and went through the initial music theory, music history classes, English literature classes. There was one semester I think I was in my sophomore year and it was all Chaucer and European motets. And I was like, I don't like this. It's not that these things are not interesting in their own right, but what about the rest of the world? And I was so frustrated that everything was so Eurocentric, and I ran around campus, and I met with all these different faculty members in different programs, the ecology professor, I met with Henry Louis Gates Jr., who was the African and African American Studies Director at the time, and I just talked to all these people and said, I want to study something else. And there was a very new field at that time, I'm dating myself but this was the late 90s, called Performance Studies. It was an interdisciplinary field that hadn't existed. Different people said, it sounds like what you're interested in is Performance Studies. So I made it my own major. I was just talking to my dad about this recently. I have a really vivid memory of looking at the front of the library with 1,000s and 1,000s of books. It's like this bastion of knowledge, or people think this is the repository of knowledge. I remember thinking that performances hold so much meaning and so much knowledge about the world and if we only think that what is written down has meaning, we're going to miss so much knowledge and meaning making, and intellectual contributions of so much of the world. There are dance practices, there are music practices, there are drama practices that are not in these books. And they thrive in oral traditions. If I only count what's in these books, I am going to be stuck with Chaucer and motets. I'm not going to learn the indigenous methods for the African American traditions or the African traditions, which is my background, because they're not in the books. There are amazing African griot traditions of oral storytelling. Those things live in performance. That's how I found my way to Performance Studies because I was not getting what I wanted. It's not in these books. I'm gonna find it in performance. I went on later in life to get a Masters and a PhD in this field of Performance Studies. But I came to that late because I really felt if you carry this idea to its logical extension, that performance has as much meaning as the written word, then you will not just write about performance, you will perform about performance and I wanted to be an artist. I found that down the line, especially in my early years in New York, and in the musical theatre circuit, it was less than I'd hoped for. There were wonderful things about it, but you didn't have Michael R. Jackson on the scene. You didn't have people thinking in such inclusive ways about the diversity, the racial inclusion. I was hard to cast. I remember going in for *Bombay Dreams* and getting a call back and being like, I'm not South Asian. Why should I be in that? I remember thinking at that time, people are not thinking as critically about creative practice in theatre and musical theatre as I would like to. And that is what sent me back to academia. I still do write scholarly works, in addition to music and lyrics, because I guess I have expanded my worldview on that. We should use all the tools at our disposal to communicate and to make change and advance the conversation in the areas that we love.

**I think this is a great thing for people to think about and read is that, arguably, there could be more intersection between where performance meets the page. You've clearly made a really, really amazing collage of a career of being able to exist in those two worlds. How much would you say that those two things existing together have influenced and made your art better?**

Well, it's so interesting, no one has asked me that. I get asked that in the other direction a lot: how does your creative practice make your scholarship better? But how does your scholarship make your creative practice better? That's a really cool question. I think there are some things that are true to both of those practices. I think you have to be curious. I think a bit of a misconception is that people think that professors and academics are know-it-alls. And some are. Probably the less interesting ones. But the ones that I aspire to be like are the ones who sustain a great curiosity about the world and are always willing to learn new things and to expand and revise their own thinking. I think that is so vital also for writing or writing for the theatre. We have to always be open. There might be a better way of doing this. I feel like there's something true to how it's done but maybe, in a certain aspect, things could shift. So that kind of curiosity and openness I think is true to both. That's a muscle. When you work on it in one space, you strengthen it for other spaces as well. I remember being in my late twenties, early thirties, and thinking my creative practice and my political views are in different spaces. There are ways that musical theatre has always been politicized or political, but it did not feel to me that the circles I was moving in, whether it be in my workshops or the musicals I was encountering, were particularly in line with my values as a person, as a person of color, as a woman. I didn't know how to bring those things together. I remember very consciously saying, I want to write in a way that brings those things together. I wound up coming out of a really wonderful workshop, The New Dramatists Composer-Librettist Studio, beginning to write the show that would wind up being the first that I wrote book, music, and lyrics for, which is a semi-autobiographical show about my mixed race family. That was the first time that I felt like I was bringing those things together. It was right around that time that I also returned to PhD studies. So I would say that another thing that my work as a critical theorist, or with critical thought, has brought to my creative practice is that it has allowed me to stand with more confidence in my thinking. I can have better tools, better language, better ways to think about certain injustices and violences in the world that scholars before me have written on, and think about how I can not just represent but honor and be true to and push against some of those things in my own musical theatre writing.

**Do you find that people seek you out for that or do you seek that out for yourself?**

It's a good question. The other thing that I should probably say is that, I'm in my forties now, I feel like I'm only just beginning as a musical theatre writer. The reason is that I had to work a day job for many years. So, for many years, I was working full time, also doing doctoral studies and writing musicals, and so the rise was very slow. And I had to make my peace with that. I would see other friends who had so many shows and I was always working on the same one slowly. So I feel like it's only just now that I'm starting to really build. I have many songs but in terms of shows, those are fewer. They've been slower to come. But, that said, I have thought about it in different ways at different times. Sometimes I have thought of it like if you're a fashion designer: you can have a line of sportswear and you can have a line of evening wear. The first show that I had staged in New York was my secret agent musical, *Sympathy Jones*, which is pure musical comedy. There is a little female empowerment and girl power to it. Some Feminism Lite maybe, and I have often thought of that as a little bit more in the commercial realm, but I think commercial tastes have also changed since when I first began. The fact that you can have shows in more commercial arenas that do tackle more challenging themes. Maybe I'm wrong, but it feels like certainly right now, in the wake of 2020, we're in a different moment. We are still going to have our *Music Man* and *Legally Blonde*. Those things are going to get produced and they're going to make money for theatres. But there seems to be, and I hope it will continue, a little bit of an appetite for something more. All that to say, I have an interest in things that are commercial and also we have to make a living. The secret agent musical didn't make a lot of money. But it gets a lot of licensed productions; it still has a life. And then I have things that I feel are more built for Off-Broadway and regional spaces. That's one way I have thought about it is, what line as a designer am I designing for? I've also realized that there are some themes across a number of the works that I have. I have a lot of shows that are about family in some way, and transnational families. I'm a lyricist of *Monsoon Wedding*: the musical which is an adaptation of the film. We're going to be rehearsing in India in the fall and performing in Qatar, and it's going to be in Brooklyn at St. Ann's in the spring. That's another show about transnational families: an American-born son who is engaged to a sort of Delhi princess in a way and, even though they are both Indian by heritage, what does that transnational situation mean for the family? There's so many things about that show that have to do with how we make sense of what our family means in spite of certain kinds of loss. That seems to be something that I return to. I think that's in my mind about my mixed race family. I did a play for Marvel about Ms. Marvel: those are some central themes to Kamala Khan and Ms. Marvel. When we did *Sympathy Jones* at the New York Musical Theatre Festival, Kate Shindle was our leading lady and she was amazing, and I had a number of writer friends there. My dad is from Ghana in West Africa, my mom is white, Scotch-Irish and Norwegian heritage. My parents had been overseas in Brazil, and I thought that they were not going to make it to the show. But they showed up one day, just surprised me and brought a lot of family members. So I had a lot of cousins, uncles and aunties in the audience. And I had a lot of African family members in the audience. And a lot of my New York-based writer friends had no idea that was my family. I just remember that there was this disconnect between my writer friends who had only ever seen me running around my little musical theatre circles, which were predominantly white at that time. There are now so many wonderful writing groups to support writers of color but they didn't exist at that time. So we were few and far between in those kinds of official musical theatre writing circles, not to say there weren't wonderful things happening in other spaces—especially at theatres that were culturally specific, but there was this kind of disconnect between who my friends thought I was and who I was with my family. And I also had some interesting experiences on that show. I thought we had written these roles that were kind of archetypal: these spies and spy characters. You know, the guys at the spy agency, villains. And I was like, you know, these roles could be played by people of any race. But when it came time to cast, a lot of people had less expansive ideas about that. And I learned from that. I remember, in particular, there were some more traditional musical comedy roles for the men and there was some resistance to thinking about actors of color in those roles. So, from that experience with *Sympathy Jones*, I realized that I wanted to write the race of the character in the script so when it came time to cast, there wouldn't be a question. So, since that time, as I've worked to bring my political values and my creative practice into clear alignment, I tend to write characters that are people of color, Black characters, and women. I tend to write a lot of women characters. Right now I'm working on this blues and gospel musical right now called *Delta Blue* that I'm writing music and lyrics for. I really valued the chance to weigh in on how this Black woman character in particular, the preacher's wife, will be represented. What kind of music she will sing, what kind of dreams she will have, what kinds of violence she will or will not be subjected to in the course of the play. I think, in some ways, that alone, just writing for characters of color and Black characters, is part of my political commitment and my through line to my creative work right now.

**What obligation do you feel like you have as a writer and composer? What obligations do you feel like you have to the future of theatre?**

The first responsibility I have is to write the best work that I can. Because I find that as a Black woman, as a woman of color, I am always asked about representation and I am rarely asked about craft. And there is a danger that people will think I'm here just to represent, not to show and use the skills that I have as an artist. So that's the first thing I would say. I have an obligation to speak about craft, which I love to do. And I have an obligation to hone my skills and to be the best craftsperson I can be. Now, that said, craft is politics, right? The fact that we think that women should sing in a certain way, or that Black characters should sing in a certain way, or that there should be a certain kind of gospel number near the close of the show. Or that, regardless of who's singing it, there can be gospel numbers even though there are no Black people in the show. These are all questions about craft and skill and maybe they're beautiful and moving in performance but are political in nature. So I have a responsibility to be the best craftsperson that I can and to encourage us to think about the craft in new and expansive ways. But I also do feel another responsibility. It's funny, I'm an introvert and I get very exhausted when press comes out. It's draining for me but some people get energized by it. It's draining for me. But I feel a responsibility to be present, and to be visible. Something as simple as buying a seat in the orchestra when I can because I want people to know that people who look like me or the people that I'm bringing with me to the theatre, can sit in the orchestra. I feel a responsibility to be present, to be visible. I do mentor rising women of color songwriters when I can, through the American Theatre Wing. I will do my best. If somebody has a question, I will really make an effort to respond or to connect them to someone who can respond because I want people to have that. I think about who I looked up to and I remember very clearly seeing Lynn Ahrens' photo in the songbook of *Once on This Island*. Seeing Lucy Simon's bio in *Secret Garden* and thinking, women do this. Women write musicals. So I know that visibility and presence is important. The other thing I would say is that I have no illusions that, because certain opportunities come to me, I am necessarily more skilled or more deserving than generations of people who came before me who did not have those opportunities. I learned this year that I was only the fifth Black woman ever to be nominated for a Tony in the category of Best Score. There had only been four before me. Micki Grant was twice nominated. Three times as many Black men have been nominated in this category. I was shocked to learn this and, in some ways, I'm surprised I was shocked. In my scholarly work, I research and write about Black women performers, and I thought that I'd have a sense of who has gotten a Tony when. I think a lot about Black women singers and how we can think about blues singers like Bessie Smith in the line of Broadway

Belters. We often think that Broadway belting began with Ethel Merman or maybe even Sophie Tucker, another great lady of song. But if you really look at who Sophie Tucker was studying with—I don't want to detract from her skills; she was a really talented Jewish singer and comedienne— but we have to understand that her voice and her persona were in conversation with the blues shouters of her time. And there's a way to sort of think about how Broadway belting comes from the blues voices. And so often people think that the blues kind of led to rock and roll and gospel. We don't usually think that blues leads to musical theatre. But, if we listen through vocal sound, it's easier to get a grasp on how that might've worked. So that's one thing I think about and I also think about which kinds of roles were available, to women in particular, when we get into the middle of the twentieth century with the first Black woman who won for Best Leading Actress in a musical, Diahann Carroll, who was playing a kind of ingénue. What did it mean to be a Black woman ingénue in that time? There are very complicated things about it; you have to be seen as kind of fragile and innocent in a way that Black women have not always been perceived in this country. The particular kind of negotiations these performers had to make. This was also at a time when we were having a rise of pop music ingénues like Aretha Franklin and Tammi Terrell, who were all performing in this very ladylike-American girls way, and serving as role models for of various different races. So it's interesting to think about. The playwright Adrienne Kennedy, who I took a class with in college, is ninety-one years old: a talented, prolific, Black woman playwright and, for the very first time, she will have a play on Broadway this coming season. She's ninety-one years old. Okay. Now I don't even know what else I can say. I also saw LaChanze this past season, in *Trouble in Mind*, which is Alice Childress' play. In 1955, it could have been on Broadway, a Black woman playwright could have been on Broadway, but they asked her to make revisions to her script and she declined. She did not want to tone down her racial commentary and so it wasn't until *A Raisin in the Sun* by Lorraine Hansberry later in the decade that a Black woman playwright's show was on Broadway. There are Black women who could have been on Broadway, whether as playwrights, as composers, as lyricists, in any category, who have not had the opportunity. I have no illusions that, when doors are cracked open for me or I find one that people forgot about and I run through it, that it's because I have more talent. I absolutely cannot believe that. I'll read you an email that Adrienne Kennedy sent me. She says:

Marvel at your immense success, Masi. You must be happy. Black women have had difficult time in past in theatre. This is astonishing.

**Amen.**

I could cry, you know. I could cry. So let's keep our wits about us. We need to know our history as we plan for the future. And I do think it's a responsibility and the deepest part of that responsibility is to be the best and most honest artist that I can.

**Thank you so much.**

# CONCLUSION

It's difficult to put a succinct summary on what you've read in the last number of pages.

Some very real truths within.

The lived experiences of people of color are complex, beautiful, ever-changing, and worthy of spending our collective time and commitment to getting closer to understanding. Never fully understanding, but getting closer to understanding. And, for our non-POC allies, the reality of never fully being able to understand a POC's existence is hard. But a realization of never fully being able to understand identities we don't live in is paramount in trying to co-exist with compassion.

Our world is not perfect. Our industry is far from perfect. But we can aim to side with good, and spend our efforts trying to get closer to that good by how we spend our energy and thought.

Learning the names of people who aren't the same as us is important. More than learning names, seeking them out is important. And, for those of us non-POC in the industry, it's important to collaborate with colleagues of Color. But it is not enough to just collaborate with us. For our non-POC allies, it's not enough to want to call us because you think you're doing something good. It's not enough to call us to want to distribute work, but not know what we do, or where our strengths lie. These are the imperfect situations that cause more harm and distress to your POC friends than good. These are the situations that make POC folks feel isolated and unseen, tokenized and frustrated.

This is a book of immensely successful, professional people. They are legends of their craft, past and present, and future. Those of us within these pages are all lucky that, while never being beyond the daily circumstances we navigate each day, being who we are, we are fairly fortunate to have reached a level of engagement in this craft where our identity creates less discomfort for those hiring us. Yet, there are so many in our industry outside of these pages whose names are still less known. There are so many professionals, both freshman and established, who still struggle to make a mark on the greater industry for reasons beyond their control. Beyond our control.

And so, I hope this book leaves you with a sense of wanting to empathize more. Of being more curious as to who the people who will *really* lead the change on the horizon will be. And a sense of trying to engage in the good work yourself. I have learned *so* much in these conversations about the immense contributions that people of color have made to this art. And I'm so proud to share a stage with them day by day.

To the younger and students reading this, and particularly our younger POC dreamers with whom the people in these pages will soon share creative space: please, please, *never* let anyone dim your light. Be humble and listen to those who have something constructive to offer, no matter who they are. *That* is being open to being moulded, and benefiting from those who are ahead of us from whom we can learn so much. But there is a line. Do not let people cross that line in a way that makes you question your self-worth. Your POC colleagues have all been there. *We have all been there.* Be smart and discern, and interpret constructive offerings in a way where you can go back to your craft, and make it so razor sharp that there is not a single wall ahead of you that you cannot cut through. The future is truly, truly yours. It belongs to all of us, but it is *especially* yours.

Isn't it exciting? The best part of all of this is that, one day, it will be impossible to write a book like this, that interviews all the shining people in our industry who identify in this way. There will be too many! Until that day, let's all continue to do our homework, strive to empathize with what we don't know, and do right by what we do in making a better mark on our art.

# IMAGE CREDITS